Rethinking Lean in Healthcare

A Business Novel on How a Hospital
Restored Quality Patient Care and Obtained
Financial Stability Using Lean

Rethinking Lean in Healthcare

A Business Novel on How a Hospital
Restored Quality Patient Care and Obtained
Financial Stability Using Lean

Thomas G. Zidel

CRC Press
Taylor & Francis Group
Boca Raton   London   New York

CRC Press is an imprint of the
Taylor & Francis Group, an **Informa** business

A PRODUCTIVITY PRESS BOOK

CRC Press
Taylor & Francis Group
6000 Broken Sound Parkway NW, Suite 300
Boca Raton, FL 33487-2742

© 2017 by Thomas G. Zidel
CRC Press is an imprint of Taylor & Francis Group, an Informa business

No claim to original U.S. Government works

Printed on acid-free paper
Version Date: 20160113

International Standard Book Number-13: 978-1-4987-7129-0 (Paperback)

Library of Congress Cataloging-in-Publication Data

Names: Zidel, Thomas G., 1949- , author.
Title: Rethinking lean in healthcare : a business novel on how a hospital restored quality patient care and obtained financial stability using lean / Thomas G. Zidel.
Description: Boca Raton : CRC Press/Taylor & Francis, 2017. | Includes index.
Identifiers: LCCN 2016000989 | ISBN 9781498771290 (pbk. : alk. paper)
Subjects: | MESH: Hospital Administration | Quality of Health Care | Quality Assurance, Health Care--methods | Efficiency, Organizational | Quality Improvement
Classification: LCC RA971 | NLM WX 150.1 | DDC 362.11068--dc23
LC record available at http://lccn.loc.gov/2016000989

Visit the Taylor & Francis Web site at
http://www.taylorandfrancis.com

and the CRC Press Web site at
http://www.crcpress.com

Contents

Foreword vii

Preface ix

Acknowledgments xi

Introduction xiii

1   The Board Meeting 1

2   The Cement That Holds Everything Together 11

3   A Not So Restful Sunday 19

4   An Unwelcomed Suggestion 25

5   Identifying Waste 41

6   A Lean Experiment 49

7   Culture Change and Systems Thinking 61

8   Status Boards 75

9   The House of Lean 89

10   Applicable Stories 97

11   Creating the Plan 109

12   Some Results 115

13   Follow-Up Board Meeting 121

14   No Time to Celebrate 135

15 Meet the New Lean Consultant 139

16 Kick-Off Meetings 145

17 Training 149

18 Staff Overview 159

19 Rounding 165

20 A Year Later 173

Index 177

About the Author 183

Foreword

The Joint Commission introduced American hospitals to quality assurance in the 1980s and to quality improvement a few years later. It also proffered its plan, do, check, act cycle as a preferred method for carrying out quality improvement activities—a method that is still widely used at present.

Well before 2000, hospitals also began to look to industry for a more comprehensive and effective approach to quality improvement and discovered Lean and Lean/Six Sigma, the methodologies through which American industries were improving their quality and enhancing their competitiveness in their home and world markets. Hospitals and health systems began to adopt both methodologies.

It has been a long process. Healthcare has been predictably slow to adopt quality improvement strategies from industry (*patients are not widgets, you know*) despite numerous well-documented, remarkable successes. Moreover, the jargon of Lean and the Japanese terms used to express its fundamental characteristics can be daunting to American hospital staff and leaders alike.

Enter *Rethinking Lean in Healthcare*. This slim book reviews and explains the principles and terms that are used in Lean for healthcare in a manner that is suitable for first-timers or those who need a refresher. It does so through the fictional account of a troubled (read, *losing money*) hospital with a somewhat hapless president and senior management staff who have learned, on their own, an important lesson—you cannot make a hospital profitable simply by cutting expenses. They are beginning to understand it but do not know what to do about it. In an intense and career-saving two-week period, however, they review their prior failures and realize that they have in front of them a potential solution to their quality problems, profitability, and dreadful staff morale: Lean for healthcare.

In a manner, this book reminds me of Berton Roueche's classic, *Eleven Blue Men*. Roueche introduced generations of physicians and nonmedical personnel to modern epidemiology through a series of engaging mystery stories that were published first in *The New Yorker* (1947–1953) and then in a compilation. The book remains enjoyable at present.

Like Roueche's stories, *Rethinking Lean in Healthcare* is a mystery. Will the hospital president survive? Indeed, can the hospital survive? What went wrong when the hospital tried Lean years earlier, and what will be different this time? What new intrigues will the team face from resistors? With his typical clarity, Zidel neatly answers all these questions while explaining how and why Lean works in healthcare. He understands how healthcare personnel struggle with certain aspects of Lean and uses his story to address those struggles in a manner that is accessible to all readers.

Rethinking Lean in Healthcare will be enjoyed by healthcare personnel and others alike while helping to disseminate an understanding of this powerful quality improvement method.

Richard Weinberg, MD CPE
Corporate director, pharmacy services, occupational medicine,
occupational and environmental safety and ergonomics,
Atlantic Health System, retired

Preface

My initial introduction to Lean manufacturing was during my tenure as a project engineer for an American multinational conglomerate in the aerospace industry. I had studied the works of Frederick Taylor, W. Edwards Deming, and Joseph Juran, but the Toyota Production System (Lean) seemed to encompass all of the principles preached by these men, and more. I became so interested in Lean that I left engineering to go and work in manufacturing. I learned from the consultants, was hired by the company, and attended countless Lean conferences. I was excited to put these principles to work. My initial experiences with Lean were not what I had hoped for. Even though the tools and principles of Lean, when applied to processes, reduced errors, increased production, improved work flow, eliminated excess inventory, and enhanced the quality of the product, the gains were not sustainable. This circumstance was extremely frustrating. I spoke with consultants and raised the question of sustainability at conferences, but the answers I received were never satisfactory. I read books on change management and experimented with the philosophies, but to no avail. The more I tried, the stouter the resistance. The company I was working for was spending huge sums of money in its attempt to become a Lean enterprise, but they were failing miserably. I knew something was missing but could not put my finger on it. I left manufacturing when I was offered an opportunity to implement Lean in healthcare. I quickly identified huge opportunities.

Unfortunately, despite everything I had heard to the contrary, the differences between manufacturing and healthcare were huge. I actually spent more time learning about healthcare than I did implementing Lean. I enjoyed healthcare much more than manufacturing, but there was still the issue of sustainability. I did, however, notice that senior leadership was more open to ideas and suggestions coming from a highly paid consultant than from their own employees. So, in 2005, I started my own consulting company (Lean Hospitals, LLC). I was convinced that the lack of sustainability was the result of Lean consultants, myself included, imposing change. So, I contracted with hospitals and other healthcare organizations to train their people in Lean tools and principles, rather than to implement the tools. The training was always well received, and the participants would leave energized and ready to implement what they had learned. Unfortunately, when I returned to these hospitals, I found the same problem; the gains were slipping away. I realized that regardless of who was imposing the change, either a consultant or management, people would resist. I was convinced that success had more to do with how the methodology was implemented than the methodology itself. So, I hit the books again! Although many of the books thoroughly described the thought process relative to Lean thinking, few talked about proper implementation. I became captivated by two questions. First, why was a company (Toyota) so willing to share its manufacturing methodology with the rest of the world? Second, why after learning the methodology did we have such difficulty duplicating Toyota's success?

This book is the story of a hospital leadership team who discovered the answers to these questions and succeeded in applying and sustaining Lean in their organization.

Acknowledgments

I thank all the people who provided input for this book:

- Pat Harris of East Jefferson General Hospital in Meterie, Louisiana, for providing the presentation *Patient Financial Services, Maximizing Reimbursement.*
- Jeremy Lyman and Deb King of Blue Mountain Hospital in Blanding, Utah, for the opportunity to take part in their fifth anniversary dinner.
- The pharmacy staff at Saint Joseph Hospital in Milwaukee, Wisconsin.
- All the people who submitted examples of successful Lean implementation that they applied at their hospitals. They were all great, and I wish that I could have fit them all in this book.

Introduction

Nick Russo is beginning his third year as the chief executive officer of a medium-sized hospital that is experiencing rumors of a takeover by a for-profit entity. Set against a backdrop of the nation's hospitals struggling to overcome financial instability, deteriorating patient care, substandard quality indicators, and waning community confidence, Nick puts his job on the line, confident that he can come up with a plan to improve the hospital's finances.

Struggling to come up with a plan, Nick's senior vice president of administrative services, Donna Castle, suggests implementing the tools and principles associated with the Toyota Production System, referred to as Lean. Donna's suggestion is forcibly rejected by the rest of the team based on their past failed experience with a Lean consultant. Rather than dismissing Donna's suggestion, Nick allows her to defend her rationalization for adopting Lean tools and principles.

This book captures the team's experiences as they move from rejecting, to accepting, to embracing the Lean culture.

Chapter 1

The Board Meeting

Nick Russo pulled into the hospital parking lot for the first Board of Governors meeting of the new fiscal year. It had rained all day, and the evening was cold, dark, and dreary, which mirrored Nick's temperament exactly. This would be his third year as the chief executive officer (CEO) of the hospital. The organization had been on a downward spiral when he took the helm, and the situation had grown progressively worse during his tenure.

He took the elevator up to the executive suite. He was surprised to see that the suite was quiet and empty when the elevator doors opened. Usually, the board members and other attendees congregate outside the boardroom before the meeting begins for informal conversations about sports, community happenings, or politics, but not today. Instead, everyone was in the meeting room, and the doors were closed. He could hear muffled conversations coming from the room, but nothing of what was being said was discernable. He stared intently at the raised panels on the polished mahogany doors and tried to prepare himself for the meeting that he knew was not going to be pleasant. Nick knew that the board members were not at all happy with his performance and that they were running thin on patience. Thus far, he had been able to keep the board members pacified with cost-cutting and revenue-enhancing ideas, which he assured them would get the organization back on track. Unfortunately, none of these tactics had produced any significant results. The hospital was losing money, the doctors were not happy, quality was at an all-time low, morale was down, and community confidence was dwindling. In addition, there were rumors that the hospital was going to be taken over by a for-profit organization, which had everyone on edge.

Nick knew that the board members would be primarily focused on the financial aspect of the organization's health. To nullify these losses, they would want to implement traditional methods to address the financial deficit. This meant more layoffs coupled with further budget cuts and program cancellations. He also knew that this approach would only exacerbate the hospital's already fragile situation. As a result of utilizing these strategies thus far, the organization was severely short staffed. His directors and managers were operating their departments on a shoestring budget, and any efforts to grow and/or improve the organization were negated due to lack of funding. The one thing he was certain of was that this approach to dealing with the organization's financial losses could not be continued. If it did, the hospital would most certainly be closing its doors.

Nick opened the boardroom's double doors and entered the room. Immediately, all conversations stopped as everyone turned and looked in his direction. There were no smiles or pleasant greetings, only silence, and an occasional look of support, or perhaps it was pity. As Nick took his seat, Dr. Mark Richardson, the chairman of the board, stared intently in his direction, slowly shaking his head without uttering a word. Nick began contemplating the possibility that, tomorrow morning, he might be scanning the *Wall Street Journal* for new career opportunities. However, he was not one to give up that easily, and he would do whatever was necessary to retain his position. Unless the board left him no choice, he was going to see this through and make the hospital profitable again.

Dr. Richardson called the meeting to order by blurting out, "Well, let's get on with this," rather vehemently, or at least it seemed that way to Nick. Kathy, Dr. Richardson's administrative assistant, read the minutes from the previous meeting, which were approved, seconded, and carried unanimously. Chairman Richardson then announced, "The board will proceed with the items on the agenda and will then move to a closed session. At the conclusion of the closed session, if the board is to take any action, such action will be taken in open session." Once again, there were glances in Nick's direction, and he felt his face tingle as the capillaries in his cheeks enlarged and his face flushed. However, he was certain the cause of his blushing was more the result of anger than embarrassment. Granted, the board members were all very successful people, but few had healthcare experience, and those who did had little business experience. The meeting proceeded with administration reports. The quality indicators were reported by Megan Casey, the chief nursing officer, and were dismal at best. Next, Joe Morgan, the chief financial officer, provided the financial report. Joe was very detail oriented, and accordingly, his reports were rather extensive. He provided what seemed to be unnecessarily lengthy reports for significant statistics, operating revenues, labor expenses, and nonlabor expenses, occasionally losing the attention of his audience. Finally, he presented the change in net assets, which was what everyone wanted to know. The hospital had lost one million, eight hundred and sixteen thousand, five hundred and seventy-nine dollars last year. This concluded Joe's presentation, and with this upsetting information hanging in the stale boardroom air, everyone turned and looked at Nick. He wasn't sure if they were looking at him because they felt he was to blame for the financial loss or because the CEO report was the next item on the agenda. He decided to believe the latter.

Nick stood up and began by discussing patient quality and safety. He spoke about monthly case reviews, coding reviews, data collection, and efforts to improve patient safety. He then moved on to operations, staff engagement, patient experience, and community partnership. For each subject matter, he provided more of the same lackluster information he had presented at previous board meetings. He knew that the board was unimpressed, but there was really nothing inspiring to report. Things were not getting better. When Nick had finished his report, Dr. Richardson asked if there were any persons wishing to address items not on the agenda. No one came forth, and with no further business, the meeting entered the closed session. Everyone who was not a member of the board was asked to leave, and as the room emptied, a few board members got up to refill their coffee cups or grab a snack.

Once the room was cleared and the board members had returned to their seats, Dr. Richardson began the closed session rather harshly, "Okay Nick, let me get right to the point. You are beginning your third year as the CEO, and quite frankly, we are less than satisfied with your performance. All the hospital indicators—finance, patient satisfaction, quality, et cetera—they are all unacceptable and getting worse. We have not seen improvement in a single area since you took the helm." Nick felt his blood boiling. His first reaction was to defend his position by identifying all the factors working against him. "This is not my fault," he thought to himself, but that was a *poor-me* approach and definitely not his style. He knew that it might not be his fault, but it was definitely his responsibility. The buck stops here! He was just about to speak when Susan Hoffman, the CEO and only surviving founder of a very successful local manufacturing company, interrupted him by saying what everyone was thinking, "We will have to have another round of layoffs."

"No!" shouted Nick somewhat instinctively. "With all due respect Susan, we cannot have another layoff. The staff is already overburdened, my managers are overwhelmed, morale is at an all-time low, and some people have already left voluntarily for more secure positions at other hospitals. More importantly, patient care is suffering. We can't just keep reducing the work force to negate our financial losses and expect it to alleviate the problems that are leading to our financial instability."

"Well, what do you suggest Nick? Do you have a plan?" asked Ray Driscoll, a retired vice president of finance for a national brand, leaning back in his seat with a smug look on his face. Ray had recommended and hoped to secure the CEO position, now held by Nick, for an old friend and colleague. However, after much campaigning by Ray, on his friend's behalf, somehow Nick managed to secure the CEO position. As a result, Ray was resentful and took every opportunity to make Nick appear incompetent.

"No Ray, no I don't," replied Nick, attempting to maintain his composure. "However, I do have some very good ideas. Although, the one thing I am certain of is that another round of layoffs should not and cannot be part of the plan. We can't lay off clinical staff, or patient care will deteriorate even more than it already has. Our support services, which include transport, environmental services, security, maintenance, central supply, and nutritional services, are barely functional. Another round of layoffs will improve the bottom line but only superficially. Consequently, all our indicators will worsen, and our problems will be carried over to the next quarter."

"Well, what are some of these good ideas that you propose?" insisted Ray.

Nick's mind was racing. He was frantically struggling to come up with something that would buy him some more time. "As I stated earlier, I have not formulated these ideas into a plan as of yet."

"So, what are you suggesting?" asked Ray leaning forward in his chair. "That we sweep our past losses under the carpet, not take any action to negate our losses for last year, and wait for you to establish and implement this plan that only exists in your head? What do you take us for? I think we need to hear your ideas so we can make an intelligent decision with regard to what action should be taken."

Nick was in a tough spot. Ray was going for his jugular, and unless Nick came up with something quickly, he could only imagine what action the board would take. "Okay, okay!" replied Nick. "Allow me to make a proposal. You give me until the end of the year with no layoffs or budget cuts, just one more year. If we do not see a significant improvement in the bottom line by then, I will tender my resignation." Everyone was shocked, including Nick himself. He could not believe what he had just said; the words seemed to come out without forethought, and he regretted saying them as soon as they left his mouth. He just put his job on the line and didn't even have a plan.

Ray Driscoll had a pleased expression on his face, the expression of a victor, but he didn't want to give Nick more time. He wanted Nick out and his friend in, and the sooner the better. So Ray went in for the kill. "Okay Nick, let me get this straight. You have no plan, the hospital is entering its fourth consecutive year in the red, all our quality indicators are down, and you want more time? Why should we give you more time? This request is ludicrous. I think we at least need to know what your plan is before granting this request."

Jim Donahue, a local real estate developer and a longtime board member, interjected, "Nick, you have put us in a diffi-cult position. I have to agree with Ray; we need to know your plan. If you're saying we are not going to reduce the work force, then what action do you recommend? You must have something in mind if you are so readily willing to put your job on the line. Tell us what the plan is so that we can decide if we should grant you the extension you're requesting."

Nick's head was spinning again. He had some ideas, but they were simply adaptations of previous attempts to improve the bottom line. He didn't have a plan, but he knew that he had to respond to Jim's question. "Well Jim, I have what I feel are some very good ideas, but I need some time to organize them into a strategy and develop a solid plan," he said, trying to buy some time. "I need time to meet with my team and formalize things, and then I can bring it to the board for approval."

Once again, Ray spotted an opportunity to make Nick look ineffective, and he was not going to let it pass. "Nick, you've known for some time that we had a board meeting scheduled for this evening. If you really do have these great ideas, why are you not prepared to present them this evening?"

Nick anticipated Ray's question and was ready for him this time. "I have been working with my team for several months, deliberating different strategies for dealing with this financial crisis, and we just recently hit on something that we feel is going to work. Unfortunately, we did not have enough time to formulate these ideas into a concrete plan. We just need time to bring them all together."

"How much time do you need?" inquired Jim in a soft voice, trying not to add to Nick's stress level.

"Give me two weeks. That should be enough time for us to establish the plan and have it ready to present for approval." He felt that two weeks was really not enough time, but if he had asked for any more, he thought the board might suspect that he didn't really have any ideas.

Before he could say another word, Chairman Richardson interrupted, "Fine, let's put it to a vote. All those in favor of granting a two-week extension on this matter and reconvening at that time to vote on Nick's request, please show agreement by raising your hand." Everyone raised his or her hand, except Ray. The chairman looked in his direction, with an expression that suggested that Ray should agree; Dr. Richardson gave him a moment to reconsider. Reluctantly, Ray lifted his hand but kept his wrist in contact with the table and rolled his eyes, indicating he was not totally in favor of granting Nick more time. Before Ray had a chance to change his mind, Richardson said, "Very well then, can I have a second?" Susan quickly seconded, and the motion was carried.

"Okay Nick, two weeks from tonight, we will review your plan," said Richardson, "and at that time, we will decide whether or not to grant your request. Unless anyone has anything further, this meeting is adjourned."

After the meeting, Nick went to his office and closed the door. The motion detector turned on the lights, which he quickly switched off manually. He sat at his desk in the dark, staring out the window at the night sky. He began to relive what had just taken place in the boardroom. "Well, you just wedged yourself between a rock and a hard place," he thought, as he gazed out the window into the darkness. Eventually, he decided that what is done is done. He could not afford to waste time dwelling on the past. Now, he needed to focus his energy on developing a plan that would address the hospital's financial dilemma. The thought crossed his mind that perhaps the next two weeks would be better spent looking for other employment, instead of trying to come up with a plan to make this place profitable. However, Nick was not a quitter, and he quickly put the thought out of his head.

He filled his briefcase, left his office, and headed to the parking lot. It began to rain again as he sat in his car without starting the engine. As the rain cascaded over his windshield, blurring his vision, he began to think about the ramifications of his actions. He had a rather hefty mortgage, tuition payments, credit card debt, and an above-average lifestyle. He had enough liquid assets to support his family for a year, should he need to find another job, but he did not want to consider that as an option. He shook himself from his reverie and started the car.

He dreaded the thought of going home and having to tell his wife about the meeting. She knew his situation at work was problematic and stressful, but he wasn't certain how she was going to react to his putting his job on the line. Nick and Judy had been married for twenty-four years and had three children. His daughters were both in private high schools. Hannah, the youngest, was a freshman, and Karen was a junior. Tony, his only son, was a sophomore at a local university. Although his wife Judy worked, it was a part-time job and only brought in enough money for miscellaneous expenses. Most of Judy's time was spent volunteering at church or in support of the extracurricular activities the girls participated in at school. He put the car in drive and slowly pulled out of the parking lot. He decided to take a longer alternate route home in an attempt to postpone the inevitable.

When Nick finally did arrive home, Judy was sitting in the living room reading. She looked up from her book and asked how the meeting went.

"Not very well," replied Nick.

"Why? What happened?" replied Judy with a very concerned tone, as she lowered her book.

"They had me cornered, and Ray Driscoll was bearing his fangs. They indicated that they were not pleased with my performance thus far and wanted to know how I planned to turn things around. They wanted a plan, and I didn't have one."

"So, how did you handle it?"

"I told them that I had some good ideas, but had not yet formulated them into a definite plan."

"And?"

"And, I asked for two weeks to create the plan, at which time I would present it to them for approval."

"Well, that doesn't sound too bad."

"The problem is I don't really have any ideas. We've tried cost-cutting, revenue enhancement, and process improvement initiatives. We've even visited successful hospitals in an attempt to understand and duplicate their business model, but nothing has worked."

"So what are you going to do?"

"I'm not sure yet. I'll meet with my executive team on Monday and see what we can come up with. You know what they say—there is wisdom in groups."

"I'm sure you'll come up with something," said Judy with a questioning expression.

"Oh, there's one other thing."

"What's that?"

"I told them that if I was not able to get the hospital back in the black by year-end, I ah…," he hesitated. "I would resign my position."

Judy sat up on the couch, her face contorted slightly as Nick's statement sank in. Then, she simply smiled and said, "Well you better get to work on that plan." This was not the reaction Nick expected. She walked over to his chair, gave him a kiss, and headed upstairs to bed. Judy had confidence in Nick and knew that if anyone could turn things around at the hospital, it would be him. Nick, however, was not so sure. He followed her up to the bedroom for what he was certain would be a long and sleepless night.

Chapter 2

The Cement That Holds Everything Together

Nick lay in bed staring at the ceiling. He glanced over at the clock on the nightstand. It was four fifty-one. He felt as though he had not slept a wink all night. Usually, on Saturday mornings, he slept in, but he knew that was not going to be the case today. He quietly got out of bed so as not to disturb Judy, and headed for the shower.

After his shower, he got dressed and headed down to the kitchen for some coffee. He was surprised to see Judy already sitting at the island in her robe, enjoying a cup of coffee and reading the news on the Internet.

"You're up early for a Saturday," is how she greeted him as he dragged himself into the kitchen.

"Couldn't sleep. I figured I might as well get up, go to the office, and see what I can get done. I hope I didn't wake you."

"Well you did, but it's fine. I wanted to get up early anyway, just not this early."

"Sorry, I was trying to be quiet."

"Oh! Before I forget to remind you, I know you have a lot on your mind right now, but I hope you didn't forget that you agreed to help at the church dinner next week."

"Church dinner? What church dinner?"

"Nick! I asked you about this a month ago and you agreed," replied Judy as she closed her laptop and turned in his direction, looking irritated. "Remember, the church is coming up on its twenty-fifth anniversary, and they decided to celebrate by providing free meals for the community. The committee decided that Mexican food would be nutritious, tasty, and easy to make. So we'll be making enchiladas. They are expecting between three hundred and five hundred people, so you can't bail on this."

"Five hundred? That's a lot of dinners to prepare."

"That's why you need to be there Nick. Please don't blow this off."

"I won't. What day is it again?"

"Wednesday. They plan on beginning to serve meals at five thirty, so we need to be there around four to help prepare."

"Okay, I'll make sure I'm there," said Nick as he kissed his wife goodbye and headed for the door.

"Don't you want something to eat before you go?" asked Judy.

"No thanks. I'll get a bite to eat in the cafeteria when I get to work." And with that, he was gone. On the ride to work, all he could think about was making five hundred meals on Wednesday. "My job is in jeopardy, the hospital is in dire straits, I need to come up with a plan to turn things around, and now I have to help prepare and serve five hundred meals. Why did I agree to do this? What was I thinking? I don't have time for this!"

Because it was a Saturday morning, things were pretty quiet when Nick walked into the hospital lobby. He knew, however, that it was just a matter of time before the emergency department (ED) would be overflowing and all the support services would be bustling with activity. Weekends in hospitals were pretty much like every other day, oftentimes even more hectic.

Before going to his office, he headed down to the cafeteria for a breakfast sandwich and a coffee. He was expecting to see employees sitting in the cafeteria before the start of their shift, enjoying breakfast and conversing with their friends, but the place was empty. Not giving it much thought, he grabbed a cup of coffee and a cinnamon roll. He really wanted a hot breakfast sandwich, but no one was working the grill. There was no one working at the cash registers either. Nick became very annoyed. He left some money near the register and walked into the kitchen expecting to see everyone sitting around, chatting. To his surprise, the kitchen was bustling with activity. Everyone was busy setting up patient breakfast trays for delivery to the units. Even Loretta Lewis, the director of nutritional services, was filling cups with coffee and stacking them up, ready to put on the patient trays. There must have been fifty cups of coffee sitting on the counter. Another worker was setting up trays with place mats, napkins, silverware, and condiments. There were two cooks at the griddle making meals to order and three workers warming plates, collecting the meals, assembling them on the trays, and placing them in the carts for delivery. Nick walked over to where Loretta was filling coffee cups and, after a cursory greeting, asked why no one was working the cash register. Without breaking stride, Loretta replied, "We don't have enough people. We've been operating the cafeteria on the honor system since the last layoff. We need everyone back here in the kitchen so we can get the trays out in time for breakfast." Nick felt a tingle of embarrassment and asked if there was anything he could do to help. "Yes, get me some more people. We can't keep this up forever, Mr. Russo. If I don't get some help, I don't know what I'm going to do." Nick knew that hiring more employees was out of the question, but he gave Loretta a wry smile and said he would see what he could do. He left the kitchen and headed up to his office.

In his office, he poured over the reams of data collected and submitted by his directors and managers for each of their individual areas of responsibility. It was required that all departments provide monthly status reports to his office.

Looking at the reports, it was quite obvious that much work had gone into creating them. Data had been collected, analyzed, and then put into some format that was easily understandable, usually charts and graphs. The reports were impressive. Most were bound and double-spaced, with lots of color graphs and illustrations. Nick was usually too busy to even look at these reports, much less study them. However, what he saw now as he went through the reports was not good, and this made him even more depressed. "What good is it to have people create these reports if I don't even have the time to look at them," he thought to himself. "These people are expending a lot of time and effort, which they don't have, to generate these reports, and they just sit in my inbox. In generating these reports, it was obvious that these department heads were looking for support from senior leadership. Instead, they never even received feedback." He came across Loretta's report in which she explained the situation in nutritional services and formally requested three additional full-time equivalents. He experienced a feeling of guilt knowing that his unawareness of her situation in the kitchen this morning only confirmed her belief that he never even looked at the reports. He continued with his review of the departmental reports for the rest of the morning and decided to take a much-needed lunch break. Rather than going out for lunch, which was his usual routine, he decided to eat in the cafeteria and perhaps have the opportunity to let Loretta know he read her report.

On the way down to the cafeteria, the elevator stopped on the fifth floor, and Sandy Johnson, a nurse, friend, and longtime hospital employee, stepped into the car looking a bit frazzled. "Hi Sandy," Nick said cheerfully as she got on the elevator. "Are you heading down to lunch? Maybe we can sit together and talk."

"I wish!" responded Sandy. "I can't remember the last time I took a lunch break. I'm heading down to the surgical unit. We ran out of gauze sponges again, and because it's Saturday, no one is working in the supply room, so I have to see if I can borrow some from another department."

"Again? You make it sound like you run out of sponges every day!"

"Well it's not always sponges!" responded Sandy, not surprised that Nick was unaware of this situation. "But every day, we run out of something and have to search high and low, or call the supply room, or get supplies from another department."

"Why don't they stock more?"

"Nick! I don't even have time to use the bathroom! I am trying to do my regular duties, but we are so short-staffed because of all the layoffs that I also have to clean rooms, change linens, stock supplies, transport patients,…. I even help nutritional services deliver and pick up meal trays! I can't take it anymore! You know, every night on my drive home, I say a little prayer that I didn't miss something that might cause harm to a patient! Because I am so busy, I feel that I lack focus. Things are not good, and I hate to say it, but I'm afraid patient care is not at the level it needs to be."

"I'm sorry, Sandy! I knew things were difficult, but I had no idea how overwhelmed you are. I hate these layoffs too, but we need…"

Sandy cut him off before he could finish, "Yeah, I know, we need to show a profit. I understand your situation Nick, and I don't blame you, but something needs to change." The elevator doors opened, and as she exited, Sandy looked over her shoulder before the doors closed, and without a trace of sarcasm, she said, "Enjoy your lunch Nick. Maybe we can talk some more, another time."

"I'd like that. Maybe we can…" and, before he could finish, the doors closed and Sandy was gone.

Nick felt sick to his stomach. The last thing he wanted to do now was eat. When the elevator reached the ground floor, instead of getting out, he hit the close door button and headed back up to his office to get back to work. He stayed late that night reviewing the reports, but at the end of the day, he was no closer to coming up with a plan than he was when he got there. As he was studying all this information, he stopped and had a realization, "I can review these reports forever, but the fact is I can't change these bad data into good data with the resources I have in place. Sandy is right! Something needs to change!" Before he left, he drafted a quick email to his senior administrators:

> All Senior Admins:
>
> There will be a meeting on Monday morning at 9:00 a.m. in my office to discuss the state of the organization. We have two weeks to create a viable plan to improve the organization's financial situation. Come prepared with suggestions and ideas. Enjoy what is left of your weekend, and I will see you ALL (no exceptions) on Monday morning.
>
> Regards,
> Nick

He pressed send, turned off the light, and locked his office door. Before leaving the hospital, he decided to conduct a brief assessment in a few departments. He started in the ED. As he approached the double doors leading to the ED, they flew open, and a tech went running down the hallway, almost knocking Nick down. Nick proceeded into the ED and walked toward the nurse's station. He felt as if he were invisible. The staff was so involved in their duties that no one even acknowledged his presence. He looked into the waiting room, and it was jam-packed with patients. It was standing room only. Some people were moaning in pain; others had obvious injuries that needed immediate attention. Families were asking when they were going to be seen, complaining that they had been waiting for hours. When he returned to the ED, it was a flurry of activity. He branded it as organized chaos, which he immediately identified as an oxymoron. He compared it to the pit at the New York Stock Exchange. Everyone knew what he or she was doing, but they were attempting to do it in the midst of everyone else trying to do the same thing. It could only be defined as organized chaos. He decided that the best thing he could do was leave, and he headed toward the doors. This time, he approached the doors with caution and spotted the same tech running back into the ED. He stood aside as the tech burst through the doors and continued on her mission, oblivious to his existence. "Maybe I should just go home," thought Nick. "I'm just going to be in the way if I stay here."

On the ride home, he did a mental review of what had occurred over the course of the day. He thought about Loretta and her staff diligently working together to provide meals for the patients, and how Sandy, and probably the entire nursing staff, had taken on additional duties to ensure that their patients received the best care possible, given the limited resources they had to work with. He considered how the ED staff worked relentlessly to deal with the onslaught of patients who filed unceasingly into the facility and how his directors and managers spent countless hours compiling reports that sat on his desk unopened. He realized that the only thing keeping the hospital from falling into total disarray was the unmitigated cooperative determination of his diminishing staff to care for their patients and do the best they could, in spite of the dire circumstances under which they were being forced to work. "My people are my greatest asset," he thought. "They are intelligent, competent, caring individuals, all willing to do whatever it takes to provide the best possible care for the hospital's patients. It scarcely seems possible that the hospital could be doing so poorly considering the dedication and work ethic of these people!"

Chapter 3

A Not So Restful Sunday

Nick was sitting at his desk in his office working when all of a sudden his door swung open and banged against the adjoining wall. Loretta Lewis stomped into his office and placed her resignation on his conference table. "I've had it!" she said. "I can't work like this anymore. I'm done! I quit!" Nick sat at his desk startled and speechless. A few seconds later, Sandy along with five other nurses barged in. "We quit too," she announced, speaking for the group, as they each placed their resignation on top of Loretta's. Nick was in shock; he looked at his doorway and saw a long line of people, all with their resignations in their hands. Each walked in and placed their individual resignations on his conference table. Eventually, the pile became so high that the documents began to spill over onto the floor. Suddenly, the building began to quake. Plaster was falling from the walls. Books were falling off his shelves, and the glass in the windows started shattering. Then, there came a blinding light. Nick sat up in bed with a jolt and saw Judy opening the drapes that blocked the sunlight, now entering the bedroom through the sliding glass doors at the foot of the bed. "Are you planning on sleeping all day, lazy bones?" she said with a smile. "Time to get up or we're going to be late for church."

"I was just having the worst dream. People were filing into my office with their resignations. They were complaining that the conditions they were being required to work under were intolerable. I just sat there dumbfounded, watching them come in, one after another, giving me their resignations and announcing that they couldn't continue to work like they have been any longer. There was nothing I could do. Then, the building began to fall apart. It was crumbling with all of us in it. That's when I woke up."

"Well, I'm sure there's some significance to that dream."

"You bet there is! It's exactly what I was thinking about yesterday on my drive home. Without these dedicated people, the hospital would most assuredly collapse. Judy, I have to do something! I have to turn the organization around. This isn't just about my job. It's not about me. This is about all the people who work at the hospital, their jobs, and their livelihood. There are a lot of people depending on me. I can't let them down."

"I'm sure you won't," said Judy with a good morning kiss. "You'll think of something. Now get out of bed and get ready for church. I don't want to be late."

Nick was a little annoyed at how Judy shrugged off the significance of his dream, but she had her own priorities. Right now, that priority was getting everyone to church on time.

After church, Nick went into his den and perused the many books on his shelves, looking for any that might provide a solution to his dilemma. He pulled down eight books, settled into his leather chair, and began reading. The books all had sections on change, excellence, culture, improvement, and leadership, but none of them provided a plan. It was all good information, but there were too many open ends to create a real plan. The books did not provide answers to all the real-world questions and scenarios that emerge when these ideas were put into practice. "What if we can't get buy-in? What if funds are not available? What if there is staff resistance? What if circumstances change?" Nick needed a solid plan, and these books were not providing one. He was getting frustrated and decided to put this predicament out of his head for a while and try to relax. However, in the back of his mind was the ever-present responsibility that he shouldered for all the hospital employees. He could see their faces and hear their voices as they worked diligently to do their jobs as best they could. He remembered the reactions of the people who had already lost their jobs: the humiliation, the anger, and the tears. Sometimes, people would blame themselves, but it had nothing to do with them. It was all about money.

He put the books back on the shelf and went into the kitchen. Judy was preparing Sunday lunch. Sunday was the only day of the week when everyone was home and they could enjoy a meal together. Judy loved Sundays, and Nick made up his mind not to ruin this one by talking about work.

After lunch, they all retired to the living room with some snacks and watched the L.A. Dodgers beat the Colorado Rockies five zip. Nick's father was a Dodgers fan, having grown up in Brooklyn, New York, and he stayed loyal to the team even when they picked up and moved to California. He passed his team loyalty on to Nick, who in turn did the same with his family. They all knew the players, the standings, and the player stats. They cheered together when the team did well, and they mourned together when they didn't. Watching the game was one of the few things they all had in common, and the game managed to take Nick's mind off of work. After the game, all three kids left the house to meet with friends for the evening.

Nick and Judy made themselves a light dinner with the leftovers from lunch. They sat in the kitchen eating without speaking. Finally, Judy broke the silence. "How are you doing Nick? Have you come up with any ideas for a plan?"

A bit surprised that Judy brought up the subject of work, Nick said, "No, not yet. I promised myself not to think about it today, but it's always in the back of my mind. I can't shake it."

"Well, that's understandable. This is a huge responsibility. Were the books any help?"

"Not really! They all have good information. The thing is, we've tried many of the ideas in these books, but they just don't seem to take hold for one reason or another. I have to come up with something that is really going to work, keeping in mind that whatever I come up with, Ray Driscoll is going to challenge. I need to have a rock-solid plan, no holes, or it's a sure thing that he will convince the board not to approve it."

"That's quite a challenge, especially given that you only have two weeks."

"I know. I'm planning on some long days and nights."

"Well, I think that relaxing tonight is not a bad idea. Let's just take it easy and not talk about it." They went into the living room, and Judy switched on the national news. Nick wasn't the least bit surprised to see that there was a segment on how hospitals were overcharging their patients for the care delivered. Then, there was another segment about a hospital that left a patient waiting in the emergency department for so long that the patient died, right there in the waiting room. "They make it sound like they did it on purpose. Hospitals are not in the business of killing people! We're in the business of caring for them. They have no idea what it takes to run a hospital. I can't stand how the media twists these stories to make us sound like a bunch of conniving, heartless demons who just want to get our hands on everyone's money." He grabbed the remote and changed the channel.

Judy hadn't realized how on edge Nick really was until this outburst and decided not to respond. They watched a couple of sitcoms, which managed to lighten his spirits. Eventually, they headed off to bed.

Nick sat up in bed perusing some more books he had on organizational change, but nothing struck a chord. The books all talked about change, how to manage change, the importance of changing the culture, and changing the organizational structure. There were even some stories about organizations that had successfully changed. Some books outlined methods for accomplishing change, such as *A Ten-Step Process,*

A Surefire Plan for Successful Change, and *Five Steps to Change Management*, but they just didn't apply to his situation. "Well, hopefully tomorrow, someone will have an idea for a plan," he thought as he kissed his wife goodnight, turned off the light, and settled down for what he was certain would be another restless night, void of sleep.

Chapter 4

An Unwelcomed Suggestion

Nick was up early on Monday morning. Surprisingly, he had an uninterrupted night's sleep, and he was looking forward to his morning meeting.

When he arrived at work, he took the elevator up to the "C-Suite" and stopped at Betty's desk for a quick review of his schedule. Betty was Nick's administrative assistant and a trusted member of his team. She had been with the hospital for almost thirty years, and she knew everyone and pretty much everything that happened in the hospital, so he wasn't surprised when she told him that she heard about what happened at the board meeting on Friday.

"What are you going to do, Nick?" she asked.

"Well, to be perfectly honest, I'm not sure. I have some ideas and I'm confident, that with some serious effort, I can come up with something good."

"Good isn't good enough," responded Betty. "You need to come up with something great. Ray Driscoll smells blood, and he's going to move in for the kill at the first opportunity." Betty had a very concerned look on her face, "Nick you're a good man. I don't want you to lose your job. If there is anything I can do, just let me know and consider it done."

"I know I can count on you Betty, and thank you. I requested a nine-o'clock staff meeting this morning. Could you check my schedule and see if I have any conflicting appointments?"

"I already took care of them. There was nothing on the schedule that was pressing or needed your immediate attention, so I rescheduled them for later in the week. I cleared two hours. I hope that's enough time."

"That sounds perfect. Also, could you call the cafeteria and have them send up coffee and some pastries for the meeting?"

"Actually, Loretta is up to her eyeballs with work, so I stopped and picked up some donuts and coffee on my way in this morning. It's all set up in your office."

"You're the best, Betty! Thank you! I may have to start calling you Radar," said Nick with a wink and a smile.

Nick went into his office, sat behind his desk, and decided to just enjoy the quiet for a few minutes. It didn't last long. Megan Casey, the chief nursing officer, knocked on his open door and walked in with two cups of coffee from Starbucks.

"Dark roast, black, just the way you like it," she said as she put one of the cups on his desk in front of him and took a seat at the conference table. Megan had an anxious expression on her face and wasted no time getting to the point, "Nick, what is this meeting about? Are we meeting to see which heads are next on the chopping block? We can't keep doing this Nick! Even if we don't let any clinical staff go, by laying off the support staff, we only increase the workload on the clinical staff. What's more, the nurses know that it is only a matter of time before the layoffs hit them. I'm afraid that more of them are going to start leaving on their own. Layoffs are not a solution, Nick. I can't afford to lose any more of my staff, and we can't keep cutting support services. They are already at bare bones…"

"Whoa!" exclaimed Nick, throwing up his hands and putting an end to Megan's tirade. "No, we are not meeting to plan layoffs. I agree with you wholeheartedly. Layoffs are not a solution. The reason for the meeting is to develop a plan so we can avoid the layoffs. We need to show an improvement to the bottom line by the end of the year, and we need to do it without reducing the work force."

"Well, that's a relief," Megan said as she exhaled the remaining air from her lungs. "So what's the plan?" she asked, with a confused look on her face.

"I don't have one," said Nick, "that's why we're having this meeting. But layoffs are off the table."

"There's no plan? You just told the board that we're not going to reduce the work force, and they're okay with that?"

"Not exactly, that's why we're meeting this morning. However, the goal is not to have any more layoffs."

"Well my staff will be relieved to hear that. I'll let them know as soon as possible so they can get back to work and put an end to all the gossip."

"No!" exclaimed Nick. "There are no guarantees that a layoff is not going to happen. First, we have to develop a plan. I have to present the plan to the board for approval, and if they approve it, then we can get the word out. We have two weeks, so start thinking of some ideas on how we are going to do this."

"Boy, Nick, this is a tall order. I'll try, but off the top of my head, I can't think of anything."

"Well, Megan, maybe once we all get our heads together, everything will come clear. Oh, and by the way, thank you for the coffee."

"My pleasure," she said with a hint of a smile as she left his office.

Nick was alone in his office once again, but not for long.

At eight forty-five, Joe Morgan, the chief financial officer, walked into the office. He was always the first to arrive for any meeting. He came early because he liked to know what was going on before anyone else. "So, how many?" he asked as he took his usual seat at the conference table.

"How many what?"

"How many people are we letting go this time?"

"We're not letting anyone go."

"Oh! How did you manage to get the board to agree to that?"

"That's not important. What we need to do is figure out how we are going to make the hospital profitable and not cut jobs."

"Wow!" exclaimed Joe, "I don't think two hours is going to be enough."

"I don't expect to do it in two hours. We have two weeks. So plan on some long hours for the next couple of weeks."

The other members of the team began to trickle in, and everyone was present at nine as requested. Betty was present at all the staff meetings to take minutes and was always the last to arrive. She closed the door behind her and took a seat at one of the chairs along the wall.

"Okay, let's get started. We have a big job ahead of us, and we have limited time," said Nick as he took his seat at the head of the table. He began by explaining to everyone that he was trying to avoid another work force reduction. He didn't give them any information with regard to the board meeting, but he was pretty certain that they all had an idea, just as Betty had. He finished by saying, "We need to identify some cost-cutting and revenue-enhancing opportunities."

Ron Lawley, the chief operating officer, was the first to speak. "Nick, I don't know where else I can cut costs. We shop around for the lowest prices for all our supplies and equipment. We've even prohibited the ordering of office supplies without the vice president's approval. I've also limited the quantity of supplies each department can have on hand. I'm open to suggestions, but I don't see much room for cutting back in my area."

Megan said, "Well, Ron, that has actually created problems for my people!"

"What do you mean?" asked Ron.

"For example, the latex gloves are so cheap that they tear when my nurses put them on. They tell me they are throwing away more gloves than they use. In addition, they are double gloving just in case one pair gets a tear. The nurses in ICU say that the gloves stick together, and when they pull them from the boxes on the wall, several other gloves will stick to the glove and fall on the floor. So they have to stop, pick them up, and throw them away."

Joe Morgan added to this discussion by saying, "My people tell me they're constantly running around looking for office supplies because by the time their requisition gets approved by their manager, director, and finally by me, they can be without supplies for two or three weeks."

"Hold on!" exclaimed Nick. "These are all important issues that need to be addressed, but I think we're getting off topic. We are not here to complain. We're here to develop a plan to make the organization profitable."

Donna Castle, the senior vice president of administrative services, said, "What about that Lean consultant we hired? Jill, Jane, or something like that?"

In unison, Megan and Joe let out audible sighs. Then Joe said, "It was Janice, Janice Brown, or as my people referred to her, Miss Not So Lean." Everyone laughed as they envisioned the paunchy, out-of-shape consultant. "Please don't even suggest bringing her back. She came here and pointed out all our problem areas, which we already knew. Then, she started doing these things she called *kaizen* events. What a disaster they were. We had to free up four to six people for an entire week so they could focus on these problem areas. Essentially, the *kaizen* event consisted of her bossing people around, telling them how to do their jobs differently. If anyone refused or gave her a hard time, she would report them. She would tell me that they were not team players, or that they should lose their jobs, and that we would never be successful if people with this kind of attitude are continued to be employed by the organization. She wanted me to fire people. She said it would demonstrate our commitment to the initiative and eliminate resistance to change."

"Wait a minute!" said Donna. "I went to a couple of those final presentations. The results of those events were actually quite impressive. Quicker turnaround times, shorter length of stays, the ability to process more patients, increased revenue, and decreased cost. It was all good, and if I'm correct, no one was fired."

"You're right. I was not about to fire people based on her recommendation, and with regard to results, the final presentations all sounded great, but the gains were never realized."

"Hold on, what are you talking about?" asked Nick.

"Oh, sorry Nick. This all happened before you came to the hospital. They hired this consultant to implement a methodology that seemed to show some promise. It was called Lean and was supposedly very successful in manufacturing. The consultant convinced us that it would work just as well in healthcare, and we believed her. It was a very bad experience. She tried to implement these improvement tools, but they didn't work because she didn't understand the processes. She used a lot of Japanese words that no one understood. Then, when we didn't see the results she promised, she blamed us for not forcing our staff to do things the way she said. The staff couldn't stand her, and they certainly were not going to do things her way, even if they did seem better."

"Were her ideas better?" asked Nick.

"I don't know," replied Joe, "we never got them off the ground. My people would say things like who does she think she is; she doesn't understand what I do, what I have to deal with, who I have to deal with, what regulatory requirements I have to adhere to, et cetera." "I think the ideas might have worked in a perfect world where everything happens in a predictable fashion. Regrettably, as we all know, nothing in healthcare is predictable. Things can change without a moments notice and can turn a perfectly manageable situation into disarray."

"Why didn't they explain those things to her?"

"They tried," interjected Megan, "but she wouldn't listen. She said it was passive resistance, and they were just making excuses. In her mind, it was my way or the highway."

"What were some of your experiences, Megan?" asked Nick.

"It was terrible. I thought my staff was going to rebel. And those Japanese words, people couldn't even pronounce them much less understand what they meant. It became a big joke. Nurses and techs were throwing these mispronounced words around as a humorous solution to every problem that came up, and everyone would laugh hysterically. That's probably the only good that came from it. It lightened things up a bit because everyone had a common enemy."

"Well maybe we were delinquent in our roles. Maybe we should have held people accountable for adhering to these changes? I've heard about Lean and I know that many hospitals have had some very positive results. Actually, they had outstanding results," suggested Nick.

"No, that's not the problem," said Ron shaking his head. "You all know me. I hold my people accountable for everything that I put in place. I did the same with Janice's changes. What I found was that they would do things the way she suggested when I was around, but if I was gone, they went right back to the way they did things originally. They prefer to stay in their comfort zone. These Japanese words and Janice's solutions just didn't make sense to them. Trying to do things the way she suggested was different and uncomfortable. So put it altogether, and you have a bossy consultant using unfamiliar terminology to implement changes that were uncomfortable. It was bound to fail. It didn't make sense. I wouldn't buy in either if it were me. To tell you the truth, I just got tired of trying to force them to change, and I let it go when I saw that none of the other departments were doing things her way."

"But the ideas and principles were sound, or at least I felt that they were," said Donna, a bit irritated by the reaction to her suggestion. "She talked about eliminating waste, improving processes, and…"

Megan interrupted her, rather defensively, "Waste? What waste? My people are flat out. They are taking care of more patients with less help! They are so overburdened that I am seeing a rise in the error rate. I can't be too hard on them about the errors because they're exhausted, yet they keep pushing forward because of their dedication to their patients. I'll tell you where the waste is. The consultant would pull my people to do these *kaizen* events leaving me short staffed! And her suggested changes were never even implemented. That's waste! A waste of time, a waste of money, and a waste of effort!"

Ron continued the defense. "My departments are already lean. We're operating at bare bones. You can't even get service in the cafeteria for breakfast because the entire staff is needed to help prepare patient trays for delivery to the units."

"You're misinterpreting it! That is not what it means to be a Lean organization. It's not about working with fewer people. It's about working with less waste," Donna retorted.

"Well, I have some waste to report," said Joe. "We had five catheter-associated urinary tract infections (CAUTIs) this month. They cost between a thousand and two thousand dollars each to treat, which is relatively inexpensive. Still, it means that this month, the cost of CAUTIs is between five thousand and ten thousand dollars. Also, CAUTIs fall into the category of a never event, which means we do not get reimbursed for the treatment. In addition, these infections can result in an extended length of stay, which means we don't have revenue-producing patients in those beds."

"Megan, what's going on?" asked Nick, annoyed at hearing about infection rates.

"Nick, the nurses are too overburdened. If they take the catheters out, they have to monitor the patient more closely and change bed pads more often. They feel they don't have enough time to allow them to do that, so they leave the catheter in, and the next thing you know, we have a CAUTI. It's so frustrating! It's a 'damned if you do, damned if you don't' scenario."

"I spoke with Sandy Johnson this weekend, so I know what the nurses are going through, but they can't jeopardize patient safety because it's inconvenient for them."

"Nick, it's not a matter of them being inconvenienced. They honestly don't have the time. My nurses are dedicated, competent, and caring people. They would never do anything to intentionally harm a patient. However, they have to prioritize their duties, and spending extra time with a patient because they removed a catheter is, unfortunately, low on the list," responded Megan, very defensively.

"I know! I didn't mean that the way it must have sounded, but we can't allow patient care to deteriorate just because we're in financial straits. We need to set up a time to talk about this in more detail. Right now, let's get back to the topic at hand. If cutting costs isn't an option, let's think of some ways to increase our revenue."

Joe jumped back into the conversation. "Generate more revenue? We can't manage to keep the revenue we are generating. These errors are causing us to lose money, and they're increasing our costs. In addition, they are making us vulnerable to legal action, which can be very expensive. It's the cost associated with poor quality, and if it is allowed to persist, we are going to be out of business!"

"Point taken! The cost of poor quality is something we definitely need to keep an eye on as we move forward. In what other areas do we experience poor quality?" asked Nick.

"Well, in addition to catheter infections, there are central line infections, surgical site infections, hospital-associated infections like methicillin-resistant *Staphylococcus aureus* (MRSA), *Clostridium difficile* (C-Diff), vancomycin-resistant enterococci (VRE), and a relatively new infection carbapenem-resistant enterobacteriaceae (CRE). There are medication errors, wrong site surgeries, ventilator-associated pneumonia or VAP, postsurgical wound infections, …; the list goes on and on," said Megan.

Joe picked up the ball from Megan. "*Staphylococcus aureus* infections are extremely costly. A recent nationwide study of patients with staph infections showed that hospital costs could amount to more than three times the average hospital costs of other patients."

"Are we experiencing all of these problems?" asked Nick.

"Yes, to some degree," responded Megan. "They don't all result in patient harm. Most are caught before then, but they should not be happening at all. We have to report all errors, determine the root causes, and implement corrective action. So, even if they don't result in patient harm or lost reimbursement, they are still costing us time and effort. In addition, these errors negatively affect our quality measures, and they can have an emotional effect on the staff."

Nick remembered Sandy's comment on the elevator that she says a little prayer on the drive home that she didn't miss something that might cause harm to one of her patients. Nick went over to the flip chart, grabbed a marker, and wrote *The Cost of Poor Quality*. "Okay," he said, "it seems that this should unquestionably be an area of strategic focus associated with the plan. We are not going to focus on reducing errors but rather on eliminating them."

"Well, mistakes are going to happen. We're all human," said Megan, matter-of-factly.

"I understand, but zero needs to be our goal. We want people to realize that even one error is too many," replied Nick. "We need everyone focused on providing the highest quality of care that they can."

"That's great!" said Megan. "But how do we focus on quality when the nurses, techs, and other clinical staff members barely have enough time to accomplish their regular duties?"

"That will be our assignment for the next meeting. That will give us all some time to do some research and generate some ideas. At the next meeting, we'll discuss ideas for improving quality. For the remainder of this meeting, I want to discuss ideas for generating more revenue."

They spent a good deal of time identifying and scrutinizing revenue-generating ideas. The majority of the ideas came with a rather hefty price tag, and Joe was given the action to calculate the return on investments for the next meeting.

"Okay, before we adjourn, does anyone have any other ideas?" asked Nick.

Donna sat up a little straighter in her chair and said, "I still want to talk about Lean. As I was saying earlier before I was interrupted, I think the ideas and principles are sound. I am not suggesting that we bring Janice back, but I think we should look at the methodology and see if it could help."

"We did that, Donna. We brought in a professional consultant, and it didn't work," countered Joe.

"Again, I am not talking about bringing Janice back. The thing is, I don't think it was the methodology that failed. I think it was her approach to implementation. Janice was trying to force people to change. She was bossy. She didn't understand how involved these processes were and made no attempt to understand them. She had a hammer, and every process was a nail. Naturally, the staff is going to resist. Actually, I'm surprised that she didn't have any major altercations with staff members."

"Oh, she did!" said Megan. "My nurses couldn't stand her, and they were not going to stand by and let her push them around. Also, I'm pretty sure that she had some run-ins with a few doctors."

"Okay," said Nick, attempting to calm things down. "We're getting off topic again." He looked at Donna and asked, "What are some of these ideas and principles that you keep referring to?"

"Well, as I was saying earlier, the definition of Lean is a system for the absolute elimination of waste." Hearing the word *waste* again, Megan let out a grunt and rolled her eyes.

"Okay, Megan. We get it. You don't like the word waste. Now, let Donna finish," said Nick, a bit irritated at Megan's behavior.

Donna continued, "There are seven categories of waste that were identified by Toyota. I can't remember all of them, but there were a few that are unquestionably related to healthcare, for example, searching. We are always searching. I believe that we could go to any department right now, and we would find someone searching for something. Another was waiting. We wait all the time. We wait for test results, for transport, for doctors, for medications.... I can go on, but I think I've made my point."

"That's true," said Nick. "When I met Sandy on Saturday morning, she was searching for gauze sponges. Joe, you just mentioned that your people are always running around looking for office supplies."

"I did, but I don't think that eliminating searching and waiting is going to make us financially stable!" exclaimed Joe, shaking his head.

"I'm not finished yet," said Donna tersely. "Granted, eliminating waiting and searching may seem trivial, but the ultimate goal is to create flow for our processes. We can't have flow if the staff is stopping to search for supplies, or charts, or medications. Nor can we have flow if they are waiting. Maybe this was a poor example, but I think we should explore the use of these principles before we dismiss them."

"I'd like to hear more about this," said Nick, "but how do you suggest we learn these principles without hiring a consultant?"

"I have the handout that Janice gave us, and I've been doing some research on the Internet. I'll make copies of the handout for the group, and if any of us find anything on the Internet that we think is valuable, we can send a link to the rest of the group."

"That sounds good for now. Betty, could you please get the handouts from Donna and make sure everyone has a copy today? I'd like everyone to study the handout, and we can discuss it at the next meeting. Unfortunately, we're out of time for today. I want to meet again tomorrow. Betty, do I have any open slots on tomorrow's schedule?"

"Sorry, Nick. I had to do some juggling of your schedule. You're booked right up until four o'clock."

"Well then, let's plan on meeting at four, and Betty, could you please coordinate everyone's schedule so that we can plan on two hours every day for the next two weeks?"

"Will do," responded Betty. "I'll set it up and make sure everyone gets the schedule, along with the handout."

"Okay, thank you everyone, and let's plan on getting together tomorrow at four."

From his desk, Nick could see Joe, Megan, and Ron standing in front of Joe's office. He assumed they were discussing Lean because they didn't seem too happy. He realized that if he did decide to adopt Lean, it was going to be a tough sell, but he hadn't made that decision yet. So he got up from his desk and closed his door so he could get on with his day.

At the end of the day, he picked up an envelope from his in-basket. It was from Betty, and inside was the handout and the meeting schedule. He quickly flipped through the handout and was immediately disappointed. There were very amateur-looking drawings that looked as though they had been drawn by a six-year-old, and most of the examples were related to manufacturing. He sighed and put it back in the envelope, filled his briefcase, and headed home.

After dinner, Nick went into his den and took out the handout. It was titled *World-Class Manufacturing*. As he flipped through the pages once again, he was a bit disappointed to see that the examples provided were related more to manufacturing processes than healthcare processes. People were referred to as operators, equipment as machines or tools, and supplies as hardware. There were also a lot of unfamiliar terms such as one-piece flow, takt time, push and pull, and standard work in process. Also, there were the Japanese words he was hearing so much about, like *muda, jidoka, heijunka, andon, poka-yoke, kaizen*, and *kanban*, none of which had any meaning to him. It was no wonder that the staff at the hospital were so put off by all of this.

"Well, I guess I should start at the beginning," he thought as he opened the first page. The section was titled *Flow Production* and included charts, diagrams, and illustrations that were incomprehensible. The section began with a story about Henry Ford. "Another manufacturing example," thought Nick. He failed to imagine how this would apply to healthcare but was determined to read on. The story explained how Ford was trying to reduce the assembly time for vehicles. In the beginning, each car was manufactured in a single location, and the workers moved from one location to the next to perform their operations. There was no set sequence to the process. Workers simply moved to whichever car was available at the time. This process was referred to as batch and queue. Ford's idea was to keep the workers stationary and move the cars so the workers could perform their process steps on one vehicle at a time. This was the birth of the assembly line and what has become known as one-piece flow. Ford's experiment reduced the manufacturing time per vehicle, from over twelve hours to just two hours and thirty minutes, with less inventory. "Now that's impressive," thought Nick, "but still, I don't see how this applies to healthcare. We're not building cars! We can't be moving patients in an assembly line."

Nick continued to read. The basic concept was that each vehicle is moved from one process step to the next in continuous flow. The assembly line at Ford Motor Company was made up of fifteen processes. The first process step was putting the wheels on the chassis, and the last step was the final assembly of the vehicle. Each interim step was laid out in the most logical sequence to ensure that everything was ready for the next step in the process. The handout claimed that by implementing one-piece flow, not only was the process faster but also there were less inventory and fewer defects. Nick leaned back in his leather chair to let this information sink in. This idea seemed to make sense, but he was still having a problem applying it to healthcare processes. He decided to read on.

The next section was a story about Toyota's executive vice president in the nineteen-fifties. His name was Taiichi Ohno. He is considered by many to be the father of the Toyota Production System, which is another name for Lean. In the story, when someone came to apply for a job at Toyota, Mr. Ohno would bring the candidate down to the production floor to observe a process in which Mr. Ohno had already observed some problems. Mr. Ohno would take a piece of chalk and draw a large circle on the floor. Then, he would tell the candidate to stand in the circle and watch until he comes back. Several hours later, Mr. Ohno would return and ask the candidate what he or she saw. If the candidate simply identified the process and the different process steps, Mr. Ohno would send him home. On the other hand, if the candidate observed problems or wasteful process steps, then he would hire the candidate.

Nick had a slight smile on his face as a quote from the New York Yankee's catcher Yogi Berra came to mind. Yogi had a knack for making statements that either didn't make sense or were blatantly obvious. This quote fell into the obvious category. Yogi said, "You can observe a lot just by watching."

Next, he reviewed the seven wastes that Donna referred to at the meeting. Donna had mentioned searching. In the handout, it was referred to as excess motion or just motion. The other waste she had identified was waiting. In addition to these two, there were transport, inventory, overprocessing, overproduction, and defects. Nick read these over a few times, attempting to memorize them, and then put the handout back in his briefcase. He decided he had reviewed enough for one night. "Tomorrow, I will do some watching and see what I observe," he thought as he left the den and joined Judy in the living room.

Chapter 5

Identifying Waste

Nick's morning consisted of one meeting after another. At ten o'clock, he had a half-hour break before his next meeting and decided to go down to one of the nursing units and do some observing. He got off the elevator and stood against the wall across from the nurse's station. Again, he felt invisible. Everyone was too busy to even notice him. A nurse walked up to the nursing station and asked the unit clerk where transport was. "I don't know," responded the clerk. "I called them three times, and each time, they said they were on the way. I'll call again."

"No, don't bother," replied the nurse. "I'll bring the patient down myself." She stomped off toward the room to get the patient.

Nick began to evaluate this situation in his mind. "The nurse is waiting, and the unit clerk made three phone calls. I think that would fall into the category of overprocessing. Now, the nurse is transporting the patient herself. I'm not sure what category that falls in. Maybe it's transport," but then he corrected himself. "No, it's excess motion." Nick noticed someone walking toward him in his peripheral vision. He turned and saw Sandy approaching.

"Hi Nick. What are you doing down here?" she asked.

"Oh, just observing. Where are you heading? Looking for supplies again?"

"Not this time. I'm heading down to the cafeteria to pick up a meal tray for a patient who missed breakfast. Loretta said she couldn't spare anyone to bring it up right away. That means it could take anywhere from twenty minutes to three hours. So, since I want the patient to have breakfast before lunch, I decided to go get it myself." The elevator doors opened, and Sandy entered and was gone.

Another set of elevator doors opened, and the transport tech came out with a transport bed. He went over to the unit clerk and asked what room the patient was in. "Oh, Nancy decided not to wait any longer and took the patient down herself."

"Why didn't you call and let us know?" inquired the transporter.

"Why didn't you come after my first phone call?" replied the clerk, a bit defensive.

"Because we're really busy!"

"Oh, and I'm just sitting here twiddling my thumbs. I'm so sorry," she responded sarcastically.

The transporter waved her off and got back on the elevator.

"Okay," mused Nick. "So now I have the waste of excess motion for the transport tech, in addition to the nurse. Also, there appears to be some animosity."

Nick then noticed a nurse behind the nurse's station searching for something. After searching for a minute or so, she looked up and asked if anyone had seen Mr. Smith's chart. With that, four people stopped what they were doing and started searching for the chart. "Wow, I just multiplied the waste by four," thought Nick.

He looked at his watch and saw that he needed to get back to his office. As he rode the elevator, he realized that he had only been on the unit for about twenty minutes, and he identified quite a bit of waste.

As he walked to his office, Betty said, "You're meeting with Dr. Snyder. She's already in your office." Dr. Snyder was the head of cardiology.

Nick thanked Betty and walked into his office. Dr. Snyder was sitting at the conference table, drumming her fingers on the tabletop. "Good morning, Carrie. What can I do for you?"

"We need to talk about... no, you need to do something about the nuclear stress tests!"

"What's the problem?"

"The problem is I get here every morning at my scheduled time, which is eight o'clock, to start conducting stress tests, and the patients are never ready. This morning, when I went down, the tech didn't even have a patient through prescan! They assure me that they will be ready at eight o'clock, and I'm lucky if I start my first test at nine. I don't get back to my office until the afternoon, so I'm not able to book any morning appointments. You need to do something about this, or I'm going to buy my own gamma camera and start doing these tests in my office. I'm serious Nick. I do three nuclear stress tests a day, and it shouldn't take me more than an hour and a half to two hours. I'm spending more than four hours every day here at the hospital because your people can't get my patients ready in time, and I can't afford that kind of time!"

"Well, don't do anything rash. Let me look into it, and I'll get back to you," replied Nick. Dr. Snyder, clearly upset, nodded, got up, and left the office. Nick asked Betty to get Asha on the phone. Asha Paswan was the director of diagnostic imaging, and he wanted to hear from her what the problem was.

When Betty had Asha on the phone, Nick picked up in his office. "Hi Asha. This is Nick Russo. Dr. Snyder was just in my office, and she is not very happy. She claims she's spending too much time here at the hospital conducting her nuclear stress tests and cannot schedule morning appointments in her office. She even threatened to buy her own gamma camera."

"I have to agree with her. The stress tests take the entire morning, and we only do three a day. I've been meaning to look at the process, but, quite honestly, I don't have the time," responded Asha.

"Not having time seems to be a common theme," said Nick as he sat down at his desk. "Have you spoken to Carol Jenkins in Process Improvement? I would think she could be of some help with this issue."

"I called her, but like everyone else, she's swamped. She said she's working on four projects that you told her were top priorities, and she has three pages of requests for assistance. So I guess I'm on page four. I'll try to get in there tomorrow morning and see what's going on."

Asha was caught totally by surprise when Nick said, "What time do the techs start? I'd like to see for myself what's happening."

"The patients arrive at seven thirty. We register them and get the ball rolling as quickly as we can."

"Okay, I'll be there at seven fifteen."

As he hung up the phone, he wondered what he would be able to do to alleviate the problem. "I don't even know all the details of doing a nuclear stress test."

It was almost four o'clock, and Joe was the first to arrive for the meeting. "Nick, I looked over Janice's handout last night, and I think this Lean idea is impractical. All the examples come from manufacturing. We've already failed at one attempt to implement, and the staff is sure to view it negatively."

"Okay, Joe. Hold your comments for the meeting. I want everyone on the same page."

When everyone was seated, Nick asked if they had a chance to review the handout. Everyone indicated that they had, and with that, he began the meeting. "Okay, let's go around and hear what you think. Joe, we'll start with you." Joe repeated the comments he made to Nick before the meeting. Megan was nodding in agreement, so Nick went to her next. "Do you have anything to add, Megan?"

"Yes, all these ideas just seem as though they are going to be additional work. There's not enough time to do the work that needs to be done. I think it will just increase the workload."

"How about you, Ron, what are your thoughts?"

"I didn't read the entire handout, but I did review the section on the seven wastes. I think I might be able to identify some areas of waste in my departments, but I don't really see this as a path to financial stability."

Nick turned to Donna. "I know you're a proponent of Lean, but would you like to add anything?"

"Yes! I agree that the examples in the handout are from manufacturing, but they are process related. We have processes here in the hospital, and I'm confident that we can apply these principles to our processes. I also agree that the staff has a negative view of Lean, but I believe that negativity is directed more toward Janice than Lean. If we explain the principles, concepts, and language to them so that they understand what it's about, I believe they will buy in. Lastly, as I stated yesterday, it is about creating flow, and in order to have flow, we must eliminate the wasteful steps in the process."

Once again, the word waste offended Megan. "I can't stand that word! There is no waste in my departments."

Nick intervened. "Actually Megan, I went up to one of your units this morning and observed quite a bit of waste in a very short time."

Megan was shocked. "What waste? Where did you identify waste?"

"Well, for example, one nurse was traveling to the cafeteria to pick up a meal tray for a patient who had missed breakfast."

"So how is that waste? That's taking care of the patient!"

"It's waste because we pay the nurses to care for the patients, not transport the patients or fetch meal trays. I could probably hire three transport techs for what we pay one nurse."

"I agree Nick, but we've let them go. There's a limited staff to do these tasks, so the nurses pick up the ball. It's not even a matter of, if you want it done right, do it yourself. It has become, if you want it done at all, do it yourself."

"Ron, transport and nutritional services are your departments. Do you have any suggestions for dealing with this problem?" inquired Nick.

"Yeah, give me some more full time equivalents (FTEs)," responded Ron, only half joking.

"Okay, we all know that's not going to happen, so let's try to come up with something useful," said Nick, annoyed by the lack of sincerity in developing a plan. All of a sudden, he had a revelation. "Wait a minute! The nurses are transporting patients, delivering meal trays, cleaning rooms, stocking supplies, et cetera. Because the nurses are picking up all these additional duties, they have less time for patient care. Since the layoffs, are we seeing an increase in the error rate? If we can show a correlation between the two, it might add some credibility to this theory."

"What theory?" asked Ron.

"The nurses are picking up additional duties because we reduced the operation's work force. As a result, errors are on the increase, which cost the hospital significant sums of money. We can hire probably three operations staff members for what it costs to hire one nurse. Perhaps we are being penny wise and dollar foolish."

"No way!" interrupted Megan. "We are not going to let nurses go so that we can hire transport techs."

"That's not what I'm suggesting. However, if we can show a correlation between layoffs and error rate, and Joe, if you can calculate the cost of these errors for last year, I might be able to convince the board…."

"Wait a minute," bellowed Joe. "You're seriously considering going to the board and asking for additional people? That'll go over like a lead balloon. You can't be serious! They want to have another layoff, and you're going to ask for additional FTEs?"

"If we can justify the dollars, then yes! Ron, I want you to determine how many FTEs you will need to get operations running smoothly. Please try to be conservative. Don't let it get out of control. Joe, I'd like you to calculate our losses due to hospital-acquired infections for last year. Megan, I'd like you to create a graph, by quarter, showing the error rate from before the layoffs to present. Okay, it's getting late, and I'm sure everyone wants to get home. What time is tomorrow's meeting, Betty?"

"Ten till noon. Would you like me to have sandwiches sent up from the cafeteria?"

"No, let's not add to Loretta's workload. She has her hands full already. Okay, I'd like everyone to review the Lean handouts again and have something positive to talk about tomorrow." With that, the meeting was adjourned, and everyone went home.

At home, Nick pulled out his copy of the Lean handout and continued reading the section on flow production. The text explained that when we batch items, several problems could arise. The processing time is longer because we are handling the same product over and over. It is easy to skip a step on one or more items depending on the size of the batch. If an error occurs, it can affect the entire batch. Finally, if an error does occur, it might not be discovered until the final inspection, in which case the entire batch will need to be reworked or scrapped. With one-piece flow, on the other hand, all the process steps are conducted on one product at a time in succession. This can be accomplished by having the item pass from one operator to the next as in an assembly line, or by one operator conducting each process step, in succession, on one item at a time.

Nick set the handout down and tried to make sense of what he just read. He tried to think of a process he could apply one-piece flow to in healthcare but was unsuccessful. He began to doubt that Lean could work in a healthcare environment.

Chapter 6

A Lean Experiment

Wednesday morning, Nick was up early so he could get to work and observe the nuclear stress test with Asha. Before he left the house, Judy reminded him about the church dinner. "We need to be there around four. Please, don't blow this off."

"I won't," replied Nick, "but right now I have to run. I don't want to be late. I'm observing a process today. I'll see you at the church tonight. Four o'clock!"

When Nick arrived at work, he headed right down to the nuclear stress test area. Asha was already waiting for him. "Good morning Nick. Thank you for offering to help with this. I really appreciate it."

"Not a problem, Asha. I read about a concept last night, and I want to see if we can apply it to this process. Also, Dr. Snyder is making threats that could affect our outpatient revenue, so I want her to know that I'm not ignoring the problem."

"Well, regardless of why you're here, I appreciate any help I can get."

"We have some time before the technologists begin processing patients. Could you have someone walk me through the process while we're waiting?"

"Sure, follow me," said Asha as she led the way into the nuclear stress test area. The area was divided into two sections separated by a curtain, which was open. On the side they entered, there were a treadmill, two desks, and two dressing rooms. On the other side was the gamma camera. A technologist was sitting at a desk next to the camera. In front of her were two large computer screens with images of someone's heart displaying the blood flow in the different chambers of the heart. Asha introduced Nick to the tech, whose name was Tammy. After some pleasantries, Asha asked her to explain the process to Nick.

"Sure, I'd be happy to," responded Tammy, as she stood and walked over to the other side of the room. She stopped at the desk closest to the entry and turned. "This is where Cora sits. Cora is the cardio tech, and she assists Dr. Snyder with the stress test. When the patients arrive, Cora brings them here to her desk to register them." Tammy then pointed to a school desk over in the corner of the room and said, "Then, the patient goes over there, and the nurse starts an IV. Once the IV is in, the patient is sent to me for a prescan," she said, gesturing toward the gamma camera. "When I finish the scan, I send the patient back to Cora, and she places the leads on the patient, brings him or her to the treadmill, and assists Dr. Snyder in conducting the stress test. After the test, Cora removes the leads and sends the patient back to me for a postscan. That's pretty much it. We do three patients a day. We start at seven thirty and are usually finished before lunch."

After thanking Tammy, Nick and Asha went out to the hallway. Nick said to Asha, "Let's get a sheet of paper and divide it into four columns. Label the columns *Cardio Tech*, *Nurse*, *Nuclear Tech*, and *Cardiologist*. Down the left-hand margin, list the time in five-minute increments, beginning at seven thirty and ending at twelve noon. Under each column heading, I want you to indicate what each person is doing during that five-minute time period."

Asha began drawing the grid as the patients arrived. At seven thirty, they expected Cora to call the first patient, but she didn't. They looked in the test area and saw Cora eating a muffin and drinking a coffee. A bit embarrassed, Asha said, "I'll let her know that the patients are ready."

Nick stopped her, abruptly saying, "No, we don't want to interfere with the process. We want to observe how the process is actually working, not the way it should work."

Asha was a bit confused but agreed to do as Nick asked. At seven thirty-five, Asha began filling out the sheet that Nick requested. For the time slot for seven thirty to seven thirty-five, under the cardio tech heading, she reluctantly wrote, *eating breakfast*. When she finished all four columns, Nick looked over her shoulder at the form. He noticed that under the nurse and cardiologist headings, she wrote, *not present*.

"Why is the nurse not here?" asked Nick.

"Oh, she works upstairs in ambulatory medicine. We page her when the patients are ready, and she comes down and does the IV," replied Asha.

"Then, she goes back to ambulatory medicine until you page her again?" asked Nick.

"Yes," responded Asha shaking her head. "It's really an inconvenience! If she's busy with a patient, for example, starting chemotherapy, we can wait twenty or thirty minutes for her to get here."

At seven forty, Cora had registered the first patient and paged the nurse. Tammy was sitting by the camera waiting, and the nurse had still not arrived. At seven forty-five, Cora and Tammy just waited. At seven fifty, Cora paged the nurse again.

"See what I mean," said Asha irritably. "I've spoken to the nurses about this, but nothing changes."

At seven fifty-five, Nick told Asha that he had to leave for a meeting. He asked her to continue collecting the information until all three patients were finished. He stressed to her that it was very important that she does not interfere with the process in any way. "Simply observe and record."

As he turned to leave, he saw Dr. Snyder walking toward them. Nick apologized straight away, "Sorry Carrie, they're not ready for you. But I want you to know that I am looking into this issue personally, and I will have it working properly by the beginning of next week."

"Well, I'm surprised to see you here," stated Dr. Snyder with a hint of sarcasm in her voice, emphasizing the word *you*. "I'm glad to see that you're taking what I said yesterday seriously. I'm losing money when I spend all morning in the hospital to conduct three tests."

"I understand, and I am handling this myself."

"Okay," replied Carrie as she turned and walked back down the hall. Without turning back toward Nick, she raised her hand over her head, with her index finger extended, and said, "One week."

Nick turned back to Asha who had a quizzical expression on her face. "You're going to have it fixed by next week?"

Nick understood her confusion and reassured her, saying "Don't worry, I have some ideas. Continue collecting the data today. When you're done, call Betty and have her set up a half-hour meeting so we can review the data together."

"Okay," responded Asha, still perplexed as to what Nick had in mind.

At ten o'clock, everyone was seated around the conference table for the crisis meeting. The crisis meeting is the name that Betty had used on the schedule. No one seemed to object, and the name stuck. Dr. Albert, the vice president of Medical Affairs, was also seated at the table. She had not been present for the previous meetings because she was out of town at a conference.

"Good morning Elizabeth," said Nick, surprised to see her. "I thought the conference ended tomorrow."

"It does, but the last day was mostly workshops, which I had no interest in, and since I don't play golf, I decided to come back early. I was concerned when I got to my office and saw a crisis meeting on my schedule, but Donna filled me in on what's going on. So I think I'm pretty much up to speed."

"Great," replied Nick. "Then let's get to work. At the last meeting, I asked everyone to review the Lean handout again and to come back with something positive. Who would like to begin?"

Megan was the first to speak. "Nick, I reviewed the handout, and I went to a few units to observe, but I'm not identifying any waste. Granted, the nurses are doing many of the tasks that would normally be conducted by support staff, but I'm having a difficult time categorizing it as waste. If I see a nurse cleaning a room or calling the pharmacy to expedite an order, I really don't think that it's waste."

"Okay," replied Nick very calmly. "Would anyone like to respond to Megan's comment?"

No one commented. Nick was beginning to get annoyed. "If you read the handout, you should remember that there are three key elements of Lean. Standard work, user..."

He was interrupted by Joe, "Yes, user-friendliness and unobstructed throughput. We did read the handout, but I don't see how it applies. I really believe that we're barking up the wrong tree with this Lean idea."

"Joe, think about it. None of these elements are in place," responded Donna. "Standard work means everyone is following the same process steps. User-friendliness means that the staff has what they need, when they need it, in the quantity it is needed. Unobstructed throughput means there are no bottlenecks. Our processes are not standardized. They're not user-friendly, and we have bottlenecks at almost every process step."

"Exactly!" said Nick. "Janice attempted to implement Lean, but as Donna just pointed out, we have none of the key components in place. Janice tried to apply the Lean tools with little or no regard for the prerequisites. There is a page in the handout that states, *without standard work, there is no continuous improvement.* I didn't get it at first, but what it means is, if people are doing things in ten different ways, it can't be measured. If it can't be measured, how do we know we've improved?"

Everyone was thinking about what Nick just said. Megan broke the silence. "Well what does that have to do with the extra duties the nurses are taking on?"

"Anyone want to answer Megan?" asked Nick.

After a brief pause, Ron said, "Everything! The nurses are performing these additional tasks because the processes are not user-friendly. If the processes are not user-friendly, we can't have unobstructed throughput. Consequently, we can't follow our standard work, and without standard work, there is no continuous improvement."

"Bingo!" said Nick. "These three elements work together. You cannot have one unless you have all three. The nurses are performing all these additional duties because our processes are not user-friendly. We need to develop standard work, make the processes user-friendly, and then make changes to eliminate obstructions to flow."

"Okay, this is beginning to make sense, but this is huge. Do you realize how many processes exist in the hospital? To apply these three components to all of these processes would be a massive undertaking. I can see this working in manufacturing where they're making one or two products. But in hospitals, we have so many different processes. It seems highly improbable!" said Joe.

Ron added to Joe's comment, "Another problem is that in manufacturing, departments can function independently of other departments. This isn't the case in healthcare. I cannot think of a single department within healthcare that doesn't either provide a service to or receive a service from another department."

Dr. Albert joined the conversation for the first time saying, "Ron is absolutely correct. A hospital is a system in which everyone should be working together for the good of the patient. I don't believe that's the case here. I believe that we operate in silos. There is a departmental focus that takes priority over everything, including the patient. It is part of our organizational culture. Directors and managers must show their value to the organization, and the only way for them to do that is by making their department appear invaluable, blameless, and effective. Unfortunately, this takes priority over the patient and is oftentimes realized at the expense of other departments."

"It seems as though every time I think I'm beginning to understand this stuff, somehow a wrench gets thrown in the works, and I'm back at square one," stated Nick, feeling somewhat dispirited.

Elizabeth responded to Nick's confusion: "Don't misunderstand me, Nick. I believe that Lean is a viable solution to the problems facing healthcare. However, it is not a quick fix. It is going to require time and a lot of hard work. What I am saying is that to be successful, we need to start by changing the organizational culture. We need the organization to function as a system. I'm referring to a system where everyone is working together for the good of the patient."

"That's all well and good, but I have to present a plan to the board a week from Friday that outlines how I am going to make the organization whole again."

"All I'm saying is that to be successful, this methodology must be implemented properly. I believe that for proper implementation, we must change the organizational culture and establish systems thinking. You mentioned earlier that Janice attempted to implement Lean with little or no regard for the prerequisites. I totally agree. However, I believe that prior to the prerequisites comes culture and systems thinking."

"Alright," said Nick as he stood up and walked over to the flip chart and wrote the words *culture and system*. "I've captured this on the flip chart, and please don't take this the wrong way Elizabeth, but we need to get back to the plan. Okay, we were talking about the three key elements and how we were going to apply them to the plethora of processes that exist within the organization. Does anyone have a suggestion?"

Megan was the first to respond. "What if we apply these elements to just one process at a time?"

Elizabeth responded, "You're missing my point. We can't apply these elements to just one process because we're a system. This is one of the reasons that most process improvement initiatives fail. Within the specified department, everything may work fine, there is buy-in, and the staff is excited about the improvements, but the support functions have different priorities. Without the support functions, the improvements cannot produce the desired results, and eventually, the improvements are abandoned."

"Why do my departments always get blamed!" said Ron, defending operations. "In my defense, many of these process improvement initiatives are conducted without representation from my departments. Then, my people receive a phone call or an email from the project leader telling them that they need to start doing something differently, and if they can't do it for one reason or another, they get blamed for the failure."

"Take it easy Ron. No one is blaming your people," exclaimed Nick. "Elizabeth is just making a point. What she's saying is, and correct me if I'm wrong Elizabeth, that we need to have representation from your departments in any process improvement initiative that is going to involve those specific departments within operations because we are a system."

"Yes, that's part of it," added Elizabeth, "but it's not that simple. In order for these initiatives to be successful, we must transform the organizational culture and build a system by eliminating silos."

Elizabeth's persistence in bringing up culture and system was exasperating. Nick replied, "We've already captured that right there on the flip chart."

"Nick, we can't simply write this on a flip chart and fool ourselves into believing it's been addressed. When you bring this to the board for approval, they're going to want to know not only what the plan is but also how you plan to successfully implement it. Keep in mind that we have tried this before unsuccessfully."

"Okay, perhaps we are getting ahead of ourselves. I have these seven wastes in the back of my head, and everywhere I go, in the hospital, I'm identifying waste. I can't wait to start implementing these Lean tools and see how they work. Regrettably, Elizabeth is right! If we don't have the culture and system in place to support these tools, they're not going to stick," said Nick.

"This whole idea seems to be getting extremely complex," said Megan. "Maybe we're in over our heads."

"I don't think we're in over our heads. I just think we need to get some structure to all of this," said Nick as he looked at the schedule. "Tomorrow, we're meeting from ten to noon. I want everyone to give some serious thought to this topic and come to the meeting with some ideas."

For the remainder of the day, Nick became so absorbed in his work that he was shocked when he looked at the clock and saw that it was three o'clock. He packed his briefcase and was stopped by Betty on his way out. "Nick, Asha called and said you wanted her to set up a half-hour meeting with you. You didn't have any open slots in your calendar, so I scheduled her for seven tomorrow morning."

"That's fine. I'll make sure I'm here on time. Sorry to cut you short Betty, but I promised Judy that I would help at the church dinner tonight, and I need to be there by four." With that, he headed for the elevator.

Nick arrived at the church at five minutes to four. He could see the relief on Judy's face from across the room. "So what are we doing?" he asked her as he greeted her with a kiss.

"Well people have been working all day preparing the ingredients. They set up an assembly line. We will be at the end of the line. When the meal comes to us, we will add some shredded cheese, ladle the sauce over the enchilada, seal the box, and bring it over to the front window where the other volunteers will be distributing the meals."

"That sounds easy enough. When do we start?"

"As soon as the meat mixture is done cooking."

Nick and Judy donned hairnets, aprons, and rubber gloves and positioned themselves at the assigned station. Nick noticed that the couples at the first few stations had already begun preparing the meals. The first station placed the tortilla in the box and added beans. The next station would add a mixture of lettuce, tomato, onions, and olives that had been previously prepared. The volunteers from the first two stations, while waiting for the meat mixture to fully cook, began to pile boxes of partially prepared meals next to the stove. The stack got so high that the boxes fell over. About five meals landed on the floor and had to be thrown out. Others had to be reassembled. "That's overproduction," thought Nick, surprised that he recognized the category of waste. He recalled a definition from the handout. *"When an upstream process continues to produce a product even when the downstream process has a backlog, it is often referred to as pushing."* These couples were pushing meals to the next process step, adding the meat mixture, even though the meat mixture was not ready. He turned to Judy and said, "They're pushing."

Judy gave him a confused look and said, "Nobody's pushing."

"No, you don't understand. They're completing their process step before the next process step is ready. Piling up unfinished meals while waiting for the next step in the process to occur creates inventory. That stack of partially prepared meals is inventory. Because the inventory was not properly managed, some of it had to be scrapped, and some required rework."

"What are you talking about? A few meals fell over. No one pushed them."

Nick realized that he might as well have been speaking in a different language, so he dropped the subject. However, the incident had piqued his curiosity, and he was suddenly excited to see how things played out.

At last, the couple assigned to work the stoves was ready to go. Nick noticed that the stoves were side by side, and the meal boxes were stacked up on their right. Every time the husband needed a meal, he would have to walk around his wife or ask her to stop what she was doing and pass one over. He remembered something in the handout about physical layout and made a mental note to read it again. At about four twenty, the meals began to come to Nick and Judy. They completed their operation, and Nick took both meals over to the window. By the time five o'clock rolled around, they had stockpiled plenty of meals ready to distribute to the community. He could hear people in the dining area complaining that their food was cold, and he noticed that the pile that he thought was sufficient was quickly dwindling. By five twenty, the stock was all gone, and people were waiting. In the kitchen, the volunteers hit the panic button. Everyone worked faster. They tried to help each other. Some meals reached Nick and Judy missing ingredients, and they had to bring them to the appropriate station to add the missing ingredients. No matter what they did, they were unable to keep up with demand. The line was growing, and people were getting irritable.

"One-piece flow!" Nick hadn't realized that he said it out loud until Judy interrupted his thought.

"What are you talking about now? Pay attention; people are waiting for a meal."

"Judy, we can get the people their meals in a steady flow if we implement a production method called one-piece flow." He stopped what he was doing and got everyone's attention. "Okay everyone, we are going to change the process. Form a line behind me. Each person will make a meal from beginning to end. Just follow me one by one." Nick picked up a box, put a tortilla inside, and spooned on some beans. He then moved to the next step, which was adding the vegetable mixture. As he did, he signaled for Judy to begin another meal. He then moved to the stove and added the meat mixture, again signaling for the next person to begin a meal. Next, he added the cheese and sauce, sealed the box, and brought it to the window. Then, he returned to the end of the assembly line.

When he got to the end of the line, he saw that there was one person at each process step, and Judy was delivering a meal to the window. "The process is flowing!" he realized with a big smile. He looked at his watch and timed how long it took for another meal to get to the window. "About thirteen seconds. We're distributing a hot meal every thirteen seconds using one-piece flow." He looked over at Judy. She shook her head and smiled. "You can be so weird sometimes, but this is working."

On the ride home, Nick kept repeating, "It works. This stuff really works."

Finally, Judy said, "Yes, I get it Nick. This stuff works. Whatever this stuff is!"

Chapter 7

Culture Change and Systems Thinking

On Thursday morning, when Nick arrived at his office, Asha was already waiting for him. "I collected all the data you asked for, but I don't see any improvement opportunities. I think the nurse is the bottleneck. I calculated that we wait one hundred and nine minutes. Eighty minutes of that is waiting for the nurse over the course of the three stress tests."

Nick took out a calculator and started punching some numbers into it. "If we take the wait time of one hundred and nine minutes and divide it by the total process time, which is four hours and twenty minutes, we get. Wow! The process efficiency is only forty-two percent."

"I'm not surprised. This is so frustrating! Waiting for the nurse really slows us down. I spoke with the nurse and her supervisor, but to no avail. They said she'll get there when she gets there. Maybe if you could talk to them, it would help."

"Okay, but first, let's take a closer look at the data." Nick noticed that during the eighty minutes of wait time, Tammy had nothing to do, and Cora filled some of the time by registering another patient. The registrations only took five minutes each. "Wait a minute. Tammy is a nuclear technologist. Doesn't she know how to start an intravenous IV?"

"Of course she does," replied Asha, "so does Cora."

"Well, why are they calling the nurse to do them?" asked Nick, baffled that something so obvious had escaped Asha's analysis of the process.

"I don't know. This is just the way we've always done it. The fact that Tammy or Cora had the training to do IVs never even occurred to me."

"So we don't need to take the nurse away from her job in ambulatory medicine," stated Nick as he continued to study the data. After a few minutes, he said, "I read about a manufacturing method called one-piece flow. I tried it last night at a church dinner with great results. Let's see if we can apply it to the nuclear stress tests. Basically, we will bring one patient through the entire process from beginning to end. Let's try to lay it out on paper."

"We can't do that. If Cora registers the patient, the nurse starts the IV, and Tammy does the prescan, Cora is going to be waiting for the prescan to end. That means Cora is waiting for the nurse and then waiting again for the prescan to end."

"Hold on!" exclaimed Nick. "I thought we just agreed that the nurse can be taken out of the process. So, Cora will register the first patient, start the IV, and then pass the patient to Tammy for prescan."

"That still doesn't make sense. If we're going to process one patient from beginning to end, Cora is going to be sitting around waiting for the prescan to end."

"Right," said Nick scratching his head. "You said the prescan is fifteen minutes. What happens next?"

Asha slid the data sheet in front of Nick. "After the scan, the patient goes back to Cora to have the leads attached. So now, Tammy has nothing to do. I don't think this is going to work, Nick."

"Let's not give up just yet. Walk me through the process again in the five-minute increments. This time, exclude the waiting and the nurse."

Asha got to prescan and was stuck. "Cora's waiting now. I can't exclude the waits."

"What if Cora registered the next patient and started the IV on that patient?"

"Then we're not bringing one patient through the process from beginning to end."

"Sure we are. The flow for the first patient hasn't been interrupted. The first patient has now finished the scan. Tammy hands him or her off to Cora who attaches the leads. While Cora is attaching the leads, Tammy begins the prescan on the second patient."

"That could work," said Asha excited about the new process. "Oh but wait. When Dr. Snyder is done with a patient, she updates the patient chart. If the next patient isn't standing on the treadmill ready to go, she'll leave. Then, we have to page her and wait for her to come back down. We can't get the leads off one patient, clean them, and put them on the next patient in that short a time."

"Then, let's buy another set of leads."

"Okay, I can do that. Oh wait, I think I may have a set of leads on another machine that we're not using."

"Great! Then, we should be all set." They walked through the process several times looking for anything they may have missed. "What do you think?" asked Nick.

"I think it just might work. I'll go downstairs and go over it with Cora and Tammy, and I'll let you know if there are any problems." Asha almost danced out of Nick's office. She was so excited.

Nick concluded his nine-o'clock meeting a little early. As the attendees filed out of his office, he saw Betty waving her phone with her hand over the mouthpiece. When she had his attention, she told him that Asha was on the phone and needed to talk with him. "She said it was very important."

Nick went to his desk and picked up the phone, anticipating some problem. "Hi Asha, this is Nick. What's up?"

"Nick, we're done!" she said.

"What do you mean, 'We're done'? Was there a problem? Did Dr. Snyder have a problem with what we were doing?" He glanced at his watch and noticed it was a few minutes before ten. His first reaction was that it didn't take long to find some holes in their improvement idea.

"No, you don't understand. We finished! All three tests are complete. Dr. Snyder came in at eight o'clock, and the first patient was standing on the treadmill waiting for her. Everything went like clockwork. She was finished at nine fifteen. An hour and fifteen minutes! She didn't say so, but I could tell she was very impressed. Also, the last patient was completely finished at nine fifty. We reduced the overall process time by two hours!"

"That's great Asha! Did you calculate the process efficiency?"

"Ninety-five percent. There was a little bit of waiting at the beginning of the process. After that, things ran smoothly."

"I wish I could have been there," said Nick a bit envious. "Well, great work and thanks for the news."

Nick couldn't wait to share his flow production experience with his team at the crisis meeting. When everyone was seated around the conference table, he conveyed his experience about implementing one-piece flow at the church dinner. Then he added, "I met with Asha early this morning, and we applied these same principles to the nuclear stress test process. She just called to give me the results. The process efficiency went from forty-two percent to ninety-five percent. The overall process time was reduced by two hours, and Carrie Snyder's time here at the hospital was reduced by two hours and fifteen minutes. Carrie didn't comment on the improvement, but I'm sure she is thrilled with these results."

"Wow! That's impressive," said Elizabeth. "However, don't expect Carrie to show any gratitude. In her mind, this is the way it should have always been."

"And she would be right. Our processes are wasteful, and nothing changes because this is the way we've always done it," said Nick. "I firmly believe that Lean needs to be our plan for moving forward and improving the hospital's finances."

"How exactly is reducing the time for nuclear stress test going to improve our finances?" asked Joe. "We don't have the volume, so we are still only doing three stress tests a day. That's not going to increase our revenue. The only person to benefit from this improvement is Dr. Snyder."

Ron jumped on this comment. "No, that's not true. We may not have the volume for nuclear, but I have a four-week backlog for regular stress tests and echocardiograms. If Cora is free now at nine fifteen, she can start doing regular stress tests and echocardiograms, which will reduce my backlog and increase our revenue. In addition, we could have easily lost the revenue generated by those three nuclear stress tests had Dr. Snyder purchased a gamma camera of her own."

"Not to mention the impact on patient satisfaction. Many of our complaints are related to wait times for tests," added Donna. "Also, we have improved physician relations."

"I think we have demonstrated two important reasons to adopt Lean. The first is that our processes are plagued with waste, and second, the tools can reduce or eliminate that waste. A week from tomorrow, I have to go before the board and present a plan for getting our finances back on track. So today, I'd like to focus on that presentation. Then we can move forward with learning more about Lean," said Nick. "So far, we have identified our key area of focus as quality. We need to demonstrate the cost of poor quality. I've asked Joe to come up with some numbers related to the cost of poor quality. Elizabeth, could you speak with Dr. Snyder and see if she would be willing to provide a statement we could use to support our decision, based on our flow production implementation in the nuclear stress test? I've also asked Ron to compile information relative to identifying the number of people necessary to get operations up and running again. That said, does anyone have ideas on how I should start the presentation? I need something that's going to pique their interest and get their attention."

Donna suggested, "How about saying, we plan to undergo a Lean transformation?"

Joe was quick to disagree. "I'm sure that rumors of our experience with Janice have spread enough that they have reached some of the board members. Even by mentioning the word Lean, we may be shooting ourselves in the foot."

"I agree," said Megan. "I think you should say something associated with our intent to focus on quality."

"The problem with that," interjected Joe, "is that quality is a cost avoidance measure. It doesn't translate directly to the bottom line. Also, quality is a proactive approach. Not to say that it is a bad thing, but it is more long term, and I'm sure the board wants quick results."

Nick was taken aback by Joe's comment but recognized its validity. "Good point Joe! The board is not looking for transformations or long-term approaches to produce results. Unfortunately, we have been so focused on finances and try-ing to cope with the situation created by our reactive approach to improving our financial situation that we have allowed our quality to diminish. We've dug a pretty deep hole, and it's not going to be easy to climb out of it."

"Well, there are no quick fixes," said Elizabeth. "Whatever we decide to do is going to take time, hard work, and commitment. I am convinced that this quality approach makes the most sense, but we need to convince the board that this is the best plan for establishing financial stability. In addition, they will need to understand that whatever we do will take time. It makes perfect sense for any organization to periodically step back and reas-sess its mission, vision, and values. We have lost sight of why we exist. Hospitals were established to care for the sick and comfort the dying. By focusing on quality, we're getting back to our roots. We need to focus on the patient and provide the highest-quality care for our patients. And we need to do it safely, effectively, efficiently, equitably, and in a timely manner."

Joe went up to the flip chart and grabbed a marker. He said, "We need to show them that our focus on finances has led us to make some bad decisions." At the top of the chart, he wrote *BAD DECISIONS* and began to list some of the methods they had employed to deal with financial instability. The list included layoffs, program cancellations, budget cuts, and postponing the purchase of new equipment.

"Okay, that's good enough for starters. Look at these four items. Do you see what they have in common? All of these things have a negative effect on quality. In addition, they prevent growth. If we don't grow the organization, we are going to be out of business in five or ten years. We need to keep up with technology, offer more and better services to our patients, hire more staff, and bring in more specialists. We are, in reality, doing the exact opposite. We cannot maintain the status quo and expect to stay in business. I think this should get the board's attention. We are caught in a vicious cycle." Joe then drew the cycle on the flip chart.

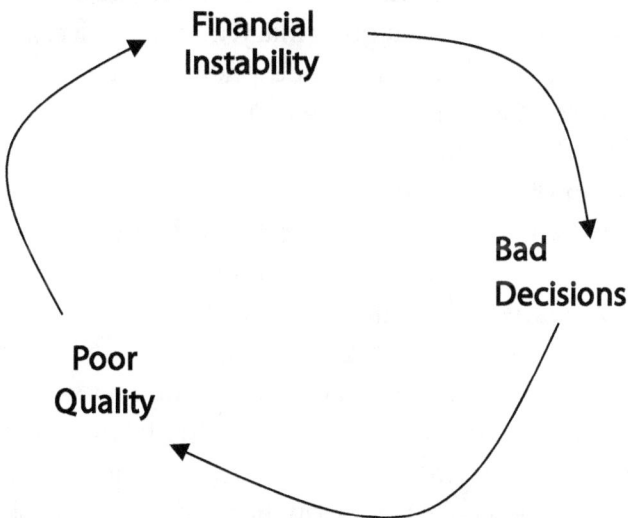

"Financial instability leads to bad decisions, bad decisions lead to poor quality, and poor quality leads to financial instability. If we remain in this cycle, we are going to be closing our doors, or we'll be bought out by a for-profit organization." Joe wrote across the top of the sheet *Reactive Cycle for Dealing with Financial Instability*. "We can show this to the board and explain how everything that we've done thus far to deal with our financial situation has had a negative effect on quality. We have the data to support this statement.

"Did you bring the data to the meeting? I haven't seen them yet," said Nick.

Joe went over to a folder and extracted copies of his data, which he passed around. "I looked at the healthcare-associated infections or HAIs for last year, and we came up with roughly four point one percent."

"That doesn't sound too bad."

"That's the problem. It doesn't sound too bad, and so we've viewed the data as acceptable, especially since the national average is between five and seven percent. We actually believe we're better than just acceptable because we're point nine percent below the national average. However, we had almost five thousand admissions last year, which equates to roughly two hundred HAIs. In the handout, you can see that I included catheter-associated urinary tract infections, surgical site infections, ventilator-associated pneumonia, central line-associated bloodstream infections, and a category I labeled as other. Then, I calculated the average cost for each category. I didn't use an overall average cost because the range is about twenty thousand dollars. For these five categories, I estimated that last year, we lost over one point eight million dollars, plus or minus a quarter of a million, just in these five categories. I haven't even looked at medication errors or medical errors. In addition, there is the cost associated with root cause analysis, corrective action, lost revenue resulting from an extended length of stay, et cetera. These costs are not captured in the average cost. The cost of poor quality is out of control, and

I'll bet you that errors have been steadily increasing since the layoffs, budget cuts, et cetera, began."

Megan said, "That can't be right, Joe. I was under the impression that our percentage was down from last year."

"Its misleading, Megan," said Joe. "The prior year, our percentage was higher at four point seven percent. The percentage was higher because we had fewer admissions and correspondingly fewer infections. So this year, we had more infections but a lower percentage. It may make sense to use proportions for quality measures, but not from a financial standpoint. Errors are on the increase, and financially it's costing us more money, regardless of what the percentages indicate. Mark Twain said there are lies, damned lies, and statistics. Statistics can be very misleading. You can't take them at face value."

Nick asked Megan if she was able to show a correlation between the number of errors and the work force reductions.

"Yes I can, but it isn't always a positive correlation. However, based on what Joe just said, maybe we should be plotting the number of errors rather than the percentage of errors."

"I agree," said Joe nodding in agreement. "With Megan's help, we can put together a graph showing a positive correlation between the rise in costs associated with poor quality and the layoffs. The layoffs started about a year before you took over Nick. So, we'll create a plot for the past three years."

"Great! Can you have that done for tomorrow's meeting?"

"If Megan is available, I'm pretty sure we can."

Megan nodded in agreement and added, "I think it is important that the board understand that the staff is working very hard and that they are dealing with very real problems. However, our flawed processes and lack of support services actually provoke errors or make it difficult to prevent them. The board needs to know that this is not a people problem. It's a processes problem. I don't want my staff blamed for these errors."

"Absolutely," agreed Nick. "Trust me on this, Megan. No one is going to blame the staff for any of our problems. This is a leadership problem, and the buck stops here. Our processes are badly broken. People have lost their jobs, and others are in jeopardy of losing theirs. The hospital is in financial straits, and the blame rests with the people sitting right here in this room. The hospital is not functioning the way it should, and we need to fix it."

Elizabeth intervened, "I think this could be a good segue into the importance of systems thinking. We can talk about silos and how they cause increased wait times for patients, communication breakdowns, obstructions to patient flow, and so on."

Nick quickly added errors and waste to that list, once again shrugging off the importance of systems thinking. Then, he said, "Alright, now comes the difficult part. Ron, how many FTEs do you think you'll need to get operations up and running again?"

Ron exhaled loudly and said, "This was a tough assignment. I'd like to bring everyone back, if they're still available and haven't found other jobs. Bringing in new people is costly and time consuming. It takes quite some time to bring them up to speed so that they are competent in their jobs. Anyway, I looked at the minimum number of people we'll need to get operations back on its feet again. I need two people in the storeroom, four in nutritional services, five in environmental services, two in maintenance—one with plumbing experience— and three in transport. That's a total of sixteen FTEs."

"How about security?" asked Nick.

"We could use some additional people in security, but maintenance helps out as needed, so I thought we could hold off on them. I felt that sixteen FTEs was a lot."

"Well, let's add two additional FTEs for security. If nothing else, it may give us some bargaining power. If we get them, then maintenance can focus on their jobs without interruption."

"Sounds good to me," agreed Ron with a glimmer of hope.

Nick then turned his attention back to Joe. "What's the average salary for these positions?"

"Including benefits, I would say about forty thousand." Joe continued talking as he did some calculations on his calculator, "we're talking a little under three-quarters of a million dollars for eighteen FTEs per year."

"Well, based on the cost of poor quality and the fact that we can show a correlation between errors and layoffs, I think we can justify bringing people back. The difficult part is going to be getting the board to agree."

"There are four categories of quality costs," said Donna. "There are prevention cost, inspection cost, the cost of internal failures, and the cost of external failures. The first two are the costs of quality. The last two are the costs of poor quality. It is a universal misconception that the cost of quality is greater than the cost of poor quality. Consequently, errors are often shrugged off as just coming with the territory. This is part of the culture change that Elizabeth mentioned earlier. The culture needs to change from one where errors are expected to one where all errors are preventable."

"So, we're back to organizational culture and systems thinking," said Nick, frustrated that they couldn't seem to get off this topic.

"Naturally, everything we try to do is going to come back to these two dynamics," said Elizabeth. "Think about it. You can't just go before the board and show them that we're losing money because of poor quality and that you plan to address the problem by hiring back people. They're going to want a plan. Saying we're going to implement Lean as an improvement strategy is not a plan, especially since we attempted to implement Lean in the past and it was such a disaster. You must convince the board members that the methodology is sound and that foregoing the critical steps of culture change and systems thinking is the reason that it wasn't successful."

"Elizabeth, how are we supposed to change the culture and eliminate silos in such a short time? Those types of changes take years!"

"You're absolutely right, but we need to start somewhere. Keep in mind that we can move forward and improve while still maintaining a focus on culture and system. Look at the nuclear stress test. Today, you experienced some very impressive results, but if we're not focused on these two dynamics, eventually, those changes will begin to wane. Right now, the only way to maintain the gain is to have Asha be vigilant in ensuring that the staff adheres to the standard work."

"Elizabeth is right," affirmed Donna. "Toyota was established in April of 1950, shortly after the end of World War II. The war had taken its toll on Japan. There were no natural resources. The country had a negative net worth, and Japan had developed a reputation for shoddy workmanship. However, what they did have was a culture. Because of the hardships they had to endure as a result of the war, the Japanese people quickly learned that they could not waste anything. This culture began in their homes and community and instinctively carried over into the workplace. Every employee working at the Toyota plants in Japan felt a sense of responsibility to eliminate waste. As a result of this culture, the Toyota Production System, or what we know as Lean, was created. In addition, doing what was honorable was also part of their culture. The honorable thing to do was to make the organization that employed them successful. This required cooperation, not competition, between departments. The point I'm trying to make is that the culture and the system did not need to be developed at Toyota. It was already deeply rooted in the employees' very being. We do not have this. So, we need to develop it."

"This is all beginning to come together," said Joe, looking at the ceiling and nodding. "I was doing some research on the Internet last night. I came across a survey conducted by a manufacturing magazine. The magazine had well over three hundred thousand subscribers. In the survey, they asked their subscribers if they had adopted Lean as their improvement methodology. Seventy percent indicated that they had adopted Lean. Next, they asked how many of these companies had achieved their anticipated results. Less than two percent answered affirmatively. Even more disturbing was the next question. They asked if these companies had experienced any improvement they would categorize as significant. Less than a quarter answered affirmatively. The reasons given for these failures ranged from lack of leadership commitment to not holding people accountable. However, based on the information that Donna just provided, I am convinced that the wrong organizational culture and the lack of systems thinking were to blame for these failures. I hadn't mentioned this information earlier because I felt it would be viewed as negativity on my part. Now, I believe it totally supports our plan. I will send everyone a link to the survey so you can look it over for yourself."

"So where do we begin?" asked Nick, convinced, yet still confused.

"We begin by changing the organizational culture. In order to get results, we need to change the culture," responded Elizabeth.

Nick stood up and walked over to his desk. He opened a search engine on his computer and typed in *organizational culture*. He got over twenty million results. He sighed and opened the first link. He read the definition and then summarized it for his team. "It defines organizational culture as a set of implied understandings that characterize an organization based on behaviors, resulting from existing beliefs, formulated by past experiences."

"Well, that's helpful," exclaimed Megan sarcastically.

"Actually, it is helpful, very helpful," countered Elizabeth. "To get results, we need to change people's behaviors. Traditionally, this is where we begin. We attempt to force people to change their behaviors. People don't oppose change, but they do oppose having change imposed on them. When we endeavor to drive people from their comfort zones, they will instinctively resist."

"What's your point?" inquired Joe.

Nick answered, "When we force change on the staff, they dig in their heels and resist. Usually, this comes in the form of passive resistance, but it's still resistance. We need to change our starting point. If their behaviors are based on beliefs, we must first change their beliefs. The only way to change beliefs is to change their experiences. If their experiences don't change, their beliefs remain the same, and consequently their behaviors remain unchanged. Hence, our improvement efforts fail. For example, on Monday, when Donna brought up Lean, there was an immediate negative response. That response was based on past experiences. Since then, successful implementation of Lean tools has changed my experiences and my perception of Lean. Accordingly, my beliefs have changed. My belief now is that Lean can transform the organization. Correspondingly, my behavior going forward will be to identify every opportunity to implement Lean tools. To summarize, to get results, we must change behaviors; to change behaviors, we must change beliefs; and to change beliefs, we must change experiences."

"How are we going to do that?" asked Joe.

"That will be the topic of tomorrow's meeting," replied Nick. He was beginning to get nervous about not having a plan ready for the board meeting. This is a lot bigger than I bargained for, he thought. He looked at Betty and asked what time tomorrow's meeting was scheduled for. She told him it was two to four. He felt a little relief knowing that they could run late if needed.

Chapter 8

Status Boards

The day seemed endless in anticipation of the crisis meeting. At ten o'clock, Nick took a trip down to nuclear medicine to see how things were working. He found Asha keeping a close eye on things, ensuring that Cora and Tammy were following the new standard work. "Elizabeth was right," thought Nick. "I'm sure that if Asha wasn't here to oversee the process, Cora and Tammy would fall back into their old routine."

Dr. Snyder was just finishing with the last patient and spotted Nick. "Good morning Nick. I have to say that things are working much better, but I'm still not totally convinced that the process is fixed. In my experience, improvement initiatives only provide temporary relief. Somehow, these processes have a way of returning to the original state of inefficiency unless they are continuously monitored by supervision. By the way, Elizabeth called and asked if I would provide a statement for the board in support of your decision to adopt Lean. I hope you understand, but I can't do that Nick for the reasons I just quantified. Maybe in a month or so, if the improvements stick, but not after only two days."

"I appreciate that Carrie," replied Nick in an understanding tone, although he was disappointed. "If at any point you see the process backsliding, please let me know right away so that I can address it."

"Oh you can count on that, but right now I have to get over to my office for my morning appointments," she smiled, winked, and headed down the hall.

The remainder of the day, Nick found himself continually distracted from the business at hand. His mind was on the crisis meeting and developing a plan for moving forward.

When the crisis meeting began, Nick delivered a quick refresher on results, behaviors, beliefs, and experiences. "So the big question is, how do we change people's experiences?"

Donna was the first to speak. "I believe that we must begin at the end and work backwards."

"No Donna!" said Nick, surprised at her statement. "I thought I made myself clear yesterday when I said we must start with experiences."

"You did! I'm referring to defining the results we want. Once we define the results, we can identify the behaviors necessary to obtain the specified results. In turn, the behaviors will describe the beliefs, and so on."

"Okay, the result we wish to achieve is to be financially stable," said Joe.

"No, it's not," retorted Megan. "The result we are striving for is high-quality patient care. If we succeed in providing great care, the finances will take care of themselves. This is what we defined as our focus on day one. Improved finances will be a benefit, but it cannot be our focus. Also, improving patient care and enhancing the patient's experience are something the staff can get fired up about. Improving finances will not get them excited. No offense Joe."

"None taken," replied Joe with a smile. "Don't you think I see that 'deer-in-the-headlights' look on people's faces when I present the financial data at the quarterly state of the hospital meetings?"

Everyone chuckled, but Nick wanted to make sure they didn't go off on a tangent, so he quickly got everyone back on track. He stood and walked over to the flip chart and wrote *Results—Quality care*. "So, the end result we are looking for is improved quality. What are the behaviors?"

Megan answered, "Putting the patient first. The patient needs to come before everything else. What Elizabeth said about getting back to our roots is key. Hospitals were established to care for the sick and comfort the dying."

"That's the desired behavior. I think we need to define what the existing behaviors are."

"I think that people are focused on what is going to make their job easier. They are taking on more and more duties, so they have less time. The CAUTI example I gave is a perfect example of this. It's easier to leave the catheter in than to remove it, even though it may result in an infection."

Nick wrote *Behavior—What's easiest*. "So what are the beliefs that lead to that behavior?"

Megan began rattling off beliefs. "The patient doesn't come first; if I want it done, I need to do it myself; things are not going to get better; my department always gets blamed; no one else does what they're supposed to do; no one cares about problems and issues; and errors come with the territory."

"Slow down Megan," interjected Nick. "Let's pick one that you feel has the greatest impact."

Megan sat in silence for a while as she reviewed all the beliefs in her head. Then, she said, "I think the belief is that leadership and management do not care about the patient. All they care about is money. My staff is stressed and frustrated, and when they try to tell someone about a problem or an issue, it falls on deaf ears. Even if someone does listen, nothing gets done because the directors and managers don't have time to address these complaints."

Nick wrote *Belief—Money takes priority over the patient*. "Does that statement sum it up?"

"Yes, I think that says it very well. Also, it links perfectly to their experiences, which I just expounded. Their experience is no one listens, and even if they do listen, nothing changes. Wait a minute. Let me rephrase that. Plenty of things change, but not for the better."

"The desired results, behaviors, beliefs, and experiences are pretty obvious now," alleged Elizabeth. "Our end result should be quality patient care. Behaviors become, do what's right. The belief, and I believe this ties into the systems thinking, is that the patient must come first. Consequently, the experiences must be that things begin to change for the better.

Nick tore off the current sheet of flip chart paper, and on a clean sheet, he wrote,

	PRESENT	*FUTURE*
Results:	Financially stable.	Quality patient care.
Behavior:	Do what's easiest.	Do what's right.
Belief:	Money takes priority over the patient.	The patient comes first.
Experiences:	Nothing improves.	Change for the better.

When he was done writing, he asked for comments.

Ron said, "Isn't that what we tried to do with Lean? We tried to change their experiences by eliminating wasteful processes steps."

"Yes, it is," said Donna, "but Janice's approach did not lend itself to success. She tried to change behaviors without first changing beliefs and experiences. She attempted to force people from their comfort zones. The outcome was mayhem, resistance, resentment, and failure. She was applying tools to processes she knew nothing about, and when people identified problems with her ideas, she dismissed their comments as resistance."

"Well, not that I'm defending her, but I can't think of anyone who knows all the intricacies of all our processes," said Joe.

"I hope you're not suggesting that we thoroughly study and understand every process before we attempt to apply Lean principles. If you are, we'll never get anything done."

Megan broke in and said, "Actually, we do have people who know all the specifics of the processes. The people who actually do the work know everything there is to know about their processes. They know the problems, and they live with these processes every day, eight hours a day, five days a week, sometimes more. Many of them have been in their jobs for ten, twenty, even thirty years. No one knows these processes better than they do. As a matter of fact, a major source of their frustration is that they have ideas that will make the processes better, but they can't get anyone to listen to them."

"Well, if they know the processes so well and have ideas to make them better, why haven't they incorporated these ideas?" asked Ron.

"For all the reasons we've been talking about. Primarily, no one listens," replied Megan. "They don't have the authority to make changes. They see the problems, they try to tell some-one, no one listens, and they get frustrated. They are at the point that they don't even try anymore. They just accept the fact that nothing is going to improve, and they simply try to make the best of their situation."

"So how is this going to work? They're going to tell us what's wrong, and we have to fix it. I don't want this inter-preted as negativity," said Ron, "but this sounds a lot like empowerment. Does anybody remember the empowerment craze in the nineties? We were going to empower people to improve the processes. They were given the authority to make changes to their processes, but the whole idea backfired. Directors and managers felt threatened, there was a lot of finger-pointing, some staff members were out of control, and others were intimidated. It was a disaster, but luckily it met with an early demise. Still, I agree with Megan that the people are the experts, but I think we need to tread very carefully here."

"So, like Lean, empowerment was another great idea that failed miserably because it was not properly implemented," said Nick. "We need to learn from these mistakes. We can't give people free reign over their processes without some guidance. The directors and managers can provide that necessary guidance. To ensure that things don't get out of control, we should establish rules. Finally, we need to develop a vehicle for the staff to alert management to problems. Keeping those things in mind, let's continue. We have identified the staff as the process experts. What we need to do now is to determine how we get them to alert management to problems they have identified."

"We could put up suggestion boxes," proposed Joe.

Ron said, "Suggestion boxes end up being a joke. No one expects any of the suggestions to be acted upon, so they make ludicrous suggestions or none at all. If we're going to use suggestion boxes, people are going to have to see results almost immediately, or they're not going to use them."

"I think the suggestion box is a good idea," said Elizabeth. "But I also agree with Ron. This is part of the culture change we are attempting to introduce. The existing culture is one that suppresses innovative thinking because people don't believe that their ideas will be adopted or implemented."

"So we need to treat every idea as important and take action to implement them, even if they seem insignificant," added Megan. "That can be our mantra; no idea is insignificant because it can change someone's experience. I do see a problem, however. Not all ideas can be implemented immediately or even in a day or two. If an idea takes more time to implement, how do we let the person who made the suggestion know that their suggestion is not being ignored?"

Donna had a suggestion: "Lean uses something called visual systems. What if, instead of a box, we used a board? We make boards that are divided into frames. Each frame represents one of the different phases of the plan, do, study, act (PDSA) cycle. If we utilize large sticky notes as suggestion forms, we can move the form from one phase to the next demonstrating that progress is being made on the submitted idea or issue. Then, the person who made the suggestion will know that their issue is not being ignored."

"What if the idea runs into a barrier and gets stuck in one phase?" asked Dr. Albert.

"Good point, Elizabeth," responded Donna with a thoughtful expression. "What if we make another frame labeled barrier? This way, the person who made the suggestion knows that their director or manager is taking action to remove the barrier."

"Won't work," said Nick as he returned to his seat. "It is not very often that a director or a manager has the authority to remove barriers to change. I think that the responsibility must fall to us, senior leadership. We will need to go around and check these boards for barriers, maybe once a week, maybe more often, maybe less often. We'll have to see what works best. Also, it won't hurt for us to be seen in the departments a little more often." Nick remembered Asha's excitement when he offered to lend some assistance with the nuclear stress test process, and he felt a little embarrassed that he hadn't made himself more accessible.

"Okay, maybe we should make an initial rough sketch of this board and work on refining it at subsequent meetings," suggested Megan, walking to the flip chart and picking up a black marker. She divided the page lengthwise and then added three horizontal lines, creating eight boxes. She labeled the boxes Suggestion, Plan, Do, Study, Act, Adopted, and Barriers. The first go-around produced a board that seemed like it might work. There was an open area on the board, so Megan labeled the box Rules. "What do you think?"

Suggestion	Plan
Do	Study
Act	Adopted
Barrier	Rules

"I think it's a good start. We may want to polish it a bit, but I think it has all the elements we need," said Donna.

"Okay, let's review and see where we are," suggested Nick. "We want to go from a focus on finance to a focus on quality. To do this, we must change behaviors from doing what is easy to doing what is right. Staff members do what is easy because they believe that the organization doesn't care about the patient. They believe that we only care about making money. So to change this belief, we must change their experiences. Up until now, staff members' experiences have been, nothing improves because no one cares. They need to have experiences that prove to them that we do care about the patient. We can change those experiences by taking actions that will improve patient care. Subsequently, we are going to create these idea boards. The boards will utilize the PDSA cycle to demonstrate that the issue is not being ignored. Finally, we are going to establish rules associated with these idea boards."

"Let's not call them idea boards," proposed Megan. "The word *idea* implies that they have a solution for resolving a problem or a better way to do something. What if they discover a problem, but they don't have a solution? Then, they may not write it on the board. I think calling them problem boards is more appropriate."

"The name *problem board* has negative implications," offered Donna. "We defined departmental focus as a primary cause of silos. Directors and managers who are determined to have their departments look good are not going to encourage their staff to highlight problems. As a matter of fact, they are more likely to discourage the practice. How about opportunity boards? Many organizations use the term opportunity rather than problem."

"Opportunity has been used so much that people know it's just another word for problem. The purpose of the board is to let people know that the issue they have identified as a problem is not being ignored. It will show the status of resolution through the four phases of the PDSA cycle and indicate if a barrier has been encountered so they know the cause of the delay. Why not just call them status boards?"

"I like that! Does anyone have an objection?" asked Nick. When no one objected, Megan wrote *Status Board* at the top of the flip chart. Nick continued, "Next, we need to establish some rules. We mentioned earlier that we are going to need some rules."

"How about no complaining!" responded Ron, only half joking.

"I think that could be misconstrued," said Megan shaking her head. "For example, we talked about how the nurses are always searching for supplies. We want to know about that because it's a form of waste. It means the process is not user-friendly. If we know the issue, we can adjust par levels, implement a process for maintaining proper supply levels, et cetera. However, the nurses may interpret not having the supplies they need as a complaint, and they don't write it on the board because it may break the 'no complaining' rule. Then, we've lost an opportunity to improve."

Ron tried again, "How about, no finger-pointing?"

"Better, but still not good. Using the same example I just gave, it could be viewed as pointing fingers at the storeroom or purchasing department. We need something generic that can't be misinterpreted."

"What if we say that it needs to be process related?" said Joe. "After all, Lean is a process improvement methodology."

"We're getting closer, but we're still not there. We will see a plethora of complaints about other departments' involvement in the process. Pharmacy is not doing this or that. Turnaround times for lab results are too long. Transport is never on time."

Ron was getting annoyed with the task and cynically exclaimed, "How about, fix your own department before looking for problems in other departments? People in glass houses shouldn't throw stones."

Megan shrugged off his comment at first but then said, "If we reword these statements, they just might be what we're looking for. It would be two separate rules. First, focus on the process, and second, stay within your area of influence. When you think about it, that's the only place the directors and managers have the authority to implement change. The rule could be stated as no crossing departmental boundaries."

Nick started writing the rules on a new flip chart page. When he had finished, he said, "Okay, we have the rules! Let's move on."

"Hold on!" interrupted Joe. "I have another rule. We are not going to purchase expensive equipment or software to solve problems or fix processes. Some people believe that purchasing new equipment or buying a new software package is the solution to every problem. They think that if we buy a new piece of equipment or update our software, everything will be better. In my experience, more often than not, when we purchase new equipment or software, it typically fails to deliver the promised outcomes. Instead of fixing a problem, the equipment or software adds complexity to the existing problem."

Nick wrote *No new equipment or software* on the flip chart and then asked if anyone had anything else to add.

"Yes, I do," stated Ron. "What if I need to refurbish or perhaps buy a new transport bed? This rule will prohibit that from happening. What if Megan needs a new IV pump?"

"I'm not referring to items like that. I'm talking about big-ticket items that cost upwards of a million dollars. Medical equipment and software can be extremely expensive."

"Then, let's say, no purchasing of expensive equipment or software."

"That's fine, but define expensive. My definition of expensive is going to be a lot different from, say, a lab tech's definition."

Nick interrupted, "Let's leave it as low cost. We can explain what we mean by low cost when we roll it out." He crossed out *No new equipment or software* and replaced it with *Low cost*. He thought about it for a minute, then, after low cost, he added *Not no cost*. "Okay, let's move on. We said that the directors and managers will be required to provide guidance. How will they know what Lean tools to apply to alleviate the highlighted problems?"

"The Japanese call them *senseis*," interjected Donna. "*Sensei* is the Japanese word for teacher. Basically, they are the experts. They possess a comprehensive knowledge of Lean tools and principles. They are the ones who provide guidance."

"Well, that exposes a huge hole in our plan. Not only are our directors and managers not *senseis*, but also we don't even have a resident expert in Lean," said Nick as he turned and looked at Donna. "You're the closest thing to an expert that we have. Any suggestions?"

"We'll have to get them training."

"There are two problems with that," said Joe. "First, how do we get all our directors and managers trained as experts? Second, who is going to do the training? I hope you're not considering Janice!"

"No, not at all. Janice didn't teach; she implemented. I remember asking her about training, and her response was that people would learn as they go. Then, she never took the time to explain anything. She just told people what to do. The closest we came to training with Janice was the handout she provided. We can't begin implementing and assume that people will learn as they go because we haven't established the correct culture yet."

"Well, that's how consultants make their money. If they come into an organization and train management, eventually, we won't need them anymore. Their engagements will be short lived, and eventually, they'll be out of business."

"I agree. So, there are plenty of books and videos on the market. Perhaps we can develop our own training."

"We don't have time for that," said Nick. "There must be people out there who conduct training. Donna, I'd like you to see if you can find someone to do that."

"Wait!" said Joe. "My first question still hasn't been answered. How do we get all of management trained as experts?"

Donna reentered the conversation. "They don't have to be experts. They just need to be familiar with the tools and principles. If we can find someone to explain the tools, give some examples, and answer their questions, then I think that is all we need."

"But then they're not experts or what did you call them, *senseis*?"

"No, they're not. However, they will become experts by applying these tools and principles. Think about it. When you graduated with your MBA, you weren't ready to become a

CFO. You needed job experience. In school, they teach you the concepts, the formulas, and the terminology. You become proficient in your field when you begin to apply what you've learned. The second rule we just identified provides an ideal environment for experimenting with Lean tools. The rule was *no crossing departmental boundaries* or *stay within your area of influence*. What can be better, it's a safe, familiar, comfortable environment where management has the authority to make changes. They can make mistakes without fear of failure. They can confirm in their own minds that Lean tools do actually work, just as Nick did with the nuclear stress test. In addition, they are sharing these experiences with their staff, so it is helping develop the new culture."

Nick stood up, "Okay, let's recap. Yesterday, we underscored the importance of culture change and systems thinking. We want to usher in a culture of providing high-quality patient care, where the patient comes first. To accomplish this, we must change behaviors by changing beliefs, which can only be accomplished by changing the staff's experiences. We have identified that a major contributor of our failed attempt at Lean implementation is endeavoring to change behaviors without first changing beliefs and experiences. Janice attempted to impose change on staff and to drive them from their comfort zone. She lacked knowledge relative to the intricacies of the processes. In addition, she failed to teach or involve the staff in the Lean methods from which these changes were derived. Based on this realization, we have identified the staff as the experts at what they do. They must be the ones to identify and implement process improvements. To accomplish this, we will empower the staff to..."

"Sorry to interrupt, Nick, but I'm concerned that the board will react negatively to the words empower or empowerment," said Ron. "I am pretty sure that most of them had some exposure to empowerment in the nineties, and more than likely, it was a negative experience."

"That's legitimate," responded Nick. "What do you suggest?"

"I started thinking about this when we were discussing culture change. You just mentioned how Janice attempted to force people to change. She incorporated intimidation tactics. This implementation method where we impose change is defined as top-down implementation. Accordingly, I think that empowerment can be defined as bottom-up implementation."

"I have to agree that bottom-up implementation does sound better. Unless someone has an objection, we'll go with that," said Nick as he continued from where he left off. "To accomplish bottom-up implementation, we will employ status boards. These boards fulfill many prerequisites required to accomplish our objectives. Not only will they provide a vehicle for staff to air their concerns and highlight issues, but also by addressing these concerns, we will be changing experiences. In addition, they provide a springboard from which we can eventually launch multidisciplinary initiatives, when the time comes. Finally, these boards provide an opportunity for directors and managers to practice and experiment with Lean tools and principles in a safe and familiar environment. Hence, they can hone their skills with Lean and become experts or *senseis*. They will be gaining the experience necessary to provide guidance for staff members to lead multidisciplinary initiatives."

"In addition, we have also established rules to prevent finger-pointing and a rule to prevent the purchasing of expensive equipment or software as solutions to problems." Nick was excited and ready to move on when he noticed Joe looking at him and tapping his watch. He looked up at the clock on the wall and noticed it was eight forty. He couldn't believe they had run over so long. "I apologize. I had no idea that it was this late. Thank you all for your help. I think we're making very good progress, and," Nick picked up the crisis meeting schedule and concluded, "our next meeting is Monday at nine. Have a great weekend, and I'll see you then."

Chapter 9

The House of Lean

Over the weekend, Nick studied the *World-Class Manufacturing* handout that Janice, the Lean consultant, had provided. One section titled *Building a Lean Organization* caught his attention. The section explained that building a Lean organization could be likened to building a house. The house depicted in the handout showed a multilevel foundation, six columns, three horizontal supporting elements spanning the six columns and supporting the roof, and of course the roof itself. Every part of the structure had a label representing a tool or concept of Lean. The house seemed tremendously complex. There was text below the house, which included many unfamiliar terms such as takt time, rightsizing, and curtain. The labels on the house included many Japanese words including *jidoka*, *heijunka*, *poka-yoke*, *kaizen*, and *kanban*, none of which had any meaning to Nick. It was no wonder that the staff at the hospital were so put off by all of these words. To make things even more confusing, there were many acronyms such as 5S, SMED, Total Preventive Maintenance (TPM), and Standard Work in Process (SWIP), which were totally foreign to him.

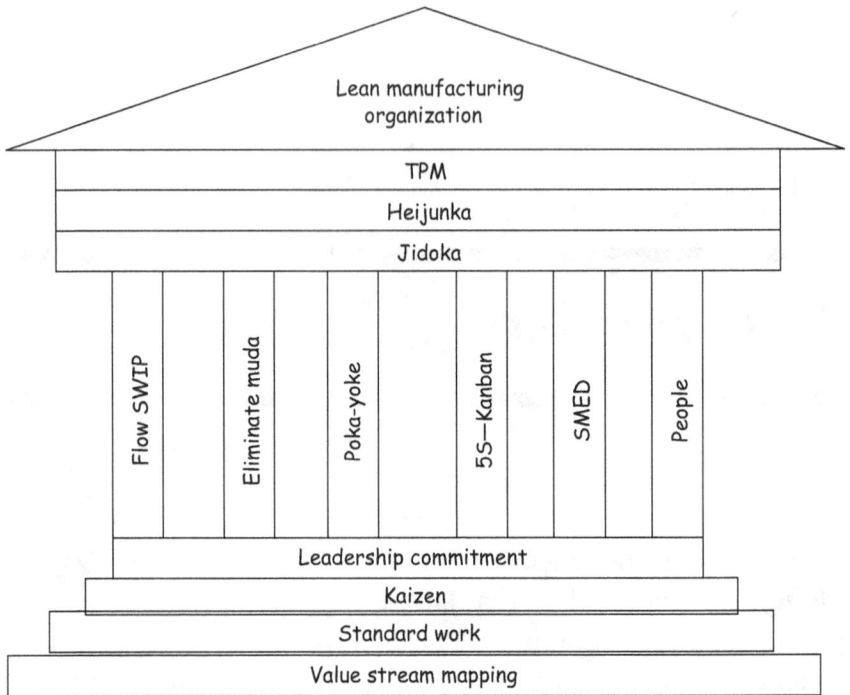

Nick decided to look on the Internet and see what information was available for these terms, acronyms, and Japanese words. He didn't find the definitions very useful or the information helpful. So instead he decided to look up "the house of Lean." He got over sixty-five million hits. "Holy cow," he thought. "There's too much information, too many variations, and too many interpretations." As he scanned through the different houses, it seemed as if there was no rhyme or reason to the different structures. "If standardization is such an integral part of Lean, they should start by standardizing the material," he said to himself out loud. He decided that it might be best to develop his own house of Lean, one that followed the rationale that he and his team had developed. He began by looking at the foundation from Janice's handout and comparing it to those on the Internet. Commitment of senior administration seemed to be pretty common. Other concepts that were common included continuous improvement, value stream mapping, a sense of urgency, teamwork, standard work, dashboards, and stability. He was convinced that the commitment of senior leadership was a necessary ingredient to the success of any change initiative. However, he did not believe it to be a foundational element for developing a Lean organization. The commitment of senior leadership, in his mind, was more of a prerequisite. Using the analogy of building a house, it would be no different from someone making the commitment to build a house and seeing it through to completion.

Of the remaining elements, he felt that only two were foundational: standard work and teamwork. Teamwork is essential for tearing down departmental silos and developing systems thinking. The more he thought about teamwork, the more he recognized that it was elusive without the right organizational culture. Culture and systems thinking are equally critical to a successful Lean transformation. However, the culture must change before the system can be established. Standard work was required for both culture change and systems thinking. He concluded that standard work should definitely be a foundational element.

Nick picked up the handout and began flipping through the pages. Ultimately, he found what he was looking for. In bold letters printed across the page was the statement, "Without standard work, there is no continuous improvement." He read it out loud and then added, "and if there is no continuous improvement, the best we can hope for is to maintain the status quo. We can't get better, we can't grow, and we won't survive." He felt he had made a big step in the right direction, but he was still only working on the foundation. "There must be more than just implementing standard work," he thought. Then, he remembered his comment at Wednesday's meeting regarding the three key elements of Lean: standard work, user-friendliness, and unobstructed throughput. He had said, "These three key elements work together. You cannot have one unless you have all three." His face lit up. He was convinced that all three key elements needed to form the foundation for his house of Lean. He recognized that everyone in the organization needed to internalize these three elements. If the staff is working on a process that does not have standard work, they need to write it on the status board. If they are required to search for supplies, or if a piece of equipment is not in working order, then the process is not user-friendly, and the staff needs to write it on the board. If standard work and user-friendliness are established, and if unexpected circumstances arise that obstruct flow, they need to write it on the board. This makes perfect sense. We are improving our processes, establishing flow, gaining experience with Lean tools and principles, changing people's experiences, and creating a new culture. The icing on the cake is that each director or manager is doing all of this in a safe, familiar environment, where they feel comfortable and can experiment with Lean tools. Then, he recognized still another benefit. "This is bottom-up implementation, which significantly increases the likelihood of sustainable and repeatable success!"

Nick felt as though he had just struck gold and began to scrutinize the supporting elements or columns. The columns in the handout were confusing, so once again he searched the Internet. Some of the houses had only two columns; others like Janice's had as many as six. Still, others didn't have any columns at all. Instead, they had building blocks. The column labels varied greatly from one house to the next. "There doesn't seem to be any consistency with this Lean methodology," he thought. "It seems as though each consulting company just made it up as they went along. It's no wonder that those manufacturing survey results displayed a ninety-eight point one percent failure rate." As he examined the different column labels, he found that the most common labels were 5S, *Poka-yoke*, Single-Minute Exchange of Die (SMED), Physical Layout, *Kanban*, and Visual Controls. Not being familiar with these terms, he began to search the web once again.

His first search was 5S. He discovered that the five S's stood for sort, straighten, scrub, standardize, and sustain. They were defined as follows:

- *Sort*—get rid of what we don't need.
- *Straighten*—organize what you keep.
- *Scrub*—clean the area.
- *Standardize*—establish standards.
- *Sustain*—maintain the gains.

"This seems like housekeeping to me," he thought. However, he questioned whether or not it should be a supporting element for a Lean enterprise. As he read the text, the association of 5S with housekeeping became greater. It was just housekeeping, but it had a supplementary benefit. The final two Ss, standardize and sustain, allowed the organization to develop the discipline necessary to follow standard work and prevent backsliding. The standard work was relatively simple. There were three rules: *if you use it, put it away; if you spill it, clean it up; and if you break it, get it fixed.* The paragraph explained that if the organization could not follow these three simple standards, it would be hard-pressed to maintain the gains necessitating adherence to the more complex standards associated with process improvements.

"5S is an important tool associated with Lean," he thought. "It has several benefits including developing the discipline necessary to become a Lean organization. Nevertheless, it is a tool. I don't believe that a tool should be a supporting element. Supporting elements should be principles or concepts." He perused the houses displayed on his computer and found one labeled *Quality.* "Now that's a supporting element," he thought. "Perhaps it should be *High-Quality Patient Care*, but that seems more like a goal than a supporting element." After some serious consideration, he decided on *Focus on Quality.*

He continued his inquiry on the Internet and found that *poka-yoke*, SMED, physical layout, *kanban*, and visual controls were all tools. He was about to abandon his search but decided to try one more. He typed *jidoka* into the search engine, a term he found on Janice's Lean handout. The definition that came up read "automation with the human touch." "Well, that's helpful," he said out loud sarcastically. There was italicized text beneath a photograph of a gentleman named Sakichi Toyoda. The text told a story of how when Sakichi was a child, his mother worked in a textile factory as a loom operator. Every day, he would watch her struggle to produce fabric on the large, heavy wooden loom. Sakichi made up his mind that when he grew up, he would invent something that would make his mother's job easier. Subsequently, in nineteen twenty-four, Sakichi invented the Type-G Toyoda automatic loom. The automatic loom had features beyond the obvious feature of it not requiring manual labor. It also had nonstop shuttle change motion and a feature that caused the machine to stop if a thread broke. The advantage of this feature was that it prevented defects. This feature spawned the concept of *jidoka*. When the machine stopped, an operator could reattach the thread and restart the machine. Therefore, instead of making a product that had to be scrapped, the machine always turned out a quality product. *Jidoka* was a form of quality control that employed four principles. First, identify the anomaly, or determine what the problem is. Next, stop the process. Don't continue processing if a defect has been identified. Third, fix the immediate problem and get the process back up and running. Finally, determine the root cause of the problem and implement countermeasures, meaning prevent the problem from reoccurring in the future if possible, or establish a method for dealing with the problem before it becomes a defect. Nick picked up his pencil and scratched out the words *quality focus* and replaced it with *jidoka*.

Nick was feeling tired and hungry but didn't want to stop, so he went to the kitchen and made himself a sandwich, grabbed a can of soda, and headed back to his den. Another supporting element on many of the houses, he observed, was *kaizen*. He was familiar with this term and knew it was derived from two Japanese words. The first was *kai*, which means change, and the second was *zen*. He, like most people, was familiar with the Japanese word *zen*, meaning for the better. *Kaizen* meant change for the better, or continuous improvement. He decided that *kaizen* should definitely be a supporting element and added it to his notepad.

He noticed that the word *people* was also a common supporting element but failed to grasp the significance. He then noticed that some of the columns were labeled "Respect for People," and this piqued his curiosity. He wondered, "Is respect for people specific to employees, patients, doctors, management, and patient families?" but quickly realized it meant everyone. He wanted to learn more about this element. Once again, he found a variety of definitions relative to respect for people, ranging from treating employees fairly to treating everyone the same. Then, he came upon yet another story about a member of the Toyoda family. The story was about former Toyota president, Kiichiro Toyoda. In June of 1950, Kiichiro was faced with a dilemma requiring either corporate restructuring, meaning a work force reduction, or the collapse of the business. For months, he fought diligently for the sake of his employees, but in the end, he realized that a layoff was unavoidable. In a gesture of respect to his employees, Kiichiro resigned his position as president. As a result of his resignation, sixteen hundred employees took voluntary retirements, and the work force reduction was no longer necessary. This act marked a new beginning for Toyota. Toyota recognized that their people were their greatest asset and went on to build a relationship of mutual trust between labor and management that continues to this day.

Nick remembered his nightmare where everyone was resigning. He became acutely aware then that without these dedicated people, the organization would most certainly collapse, but he never revisited this realization. "We need to treat these people with genuine respect. Recognizing that they are the experts at their jobs is a great start, but we need to do more. We must invest in them, develop their skills, and acknowledge their accomplishments." Nick added "Respect for People" as the third pillar. "That should do it," he said to himself, as he turned off his computer and cleaned up his desk.

Chapter 10

Applicable Stories

Monday morning, Nick arrived in the hospital parking lot at the same time as Donna. "Good morning, Donna," he said as she was getting out of her car. "How was your weekend?"

"It was okay, but nothing to write home about. I spent most of the weekend reading books and surfing the web, trying to learn more about Lean. It's all pretty confusing. Hardly anything you read is consistent from one source to the next. The words are the same, the tools are the same, but the explanations vary significantly. I did find an interesting piece, not specific to Lean, but it does support our idea about bottom-up implementation. I'll save it for the meeting this morning."

"I spent the entire day on Saturday doing the same thing. I think I have some good information for the meeting, also." They entered the hospital together, making small talk. Nick left Donna at the elevator and said, "I'll see you at the meeting. I want to go down and check the nuclear stress test process."

When Nick arrived in the stress test area, he saw Asha, and she seemed irritated about something. "Good morning, Asha. How is everything going?"

"Oh, hi Nick. I didn't see you coming. Things are going fine now, but only because I was here. Earlier, I heard a page for the nurse to report to the nuclear stress test. Cora and Tammy had reverted back to their old process, expecting the nurse to come down and start the IV. When I came into the area and asked why they paged the nurse, they acted confused. Cora said she thought we were just trying out the new process. When I told her that it was the new standard work, she got pretty upset. This is always the way it is, Nick. People just want to do what they've always done, and when you try to make things better, you get attitude."

"Hmm, that does present a problem. Listen, Asha. Monitor the process today and have Betty set up a meeting for the four of us, Tammy, Cora, you, and me, sometime this afternoon. Let's try to identify the issues and see if we can work through them."

"Okay Nick, and thanks again for your help. This can really be frustrating."

Nick went to his office where he had a short meeting with the gastroenterologists about scheduling the endoscopy suites to better fit their schedules. He promised to look into it and made a note in his planner.

At nine o'clock, the crisis meeting was ready to begin. Everyone seemed anxious to get going, and Nick was looking forward to seeing what they had discovered over the weekend.

"Okay, let's get started. I believe that Donna has something to share, so let's start with her."

Donna passed out copies of the nine pages she had printed off the Internet. "This website tells a story about a guy named Jerry Sternin. I will summarize it, but I suggest you each read it in its entirety when you get a chance. In nineteen-ninety, Save the Children sent Jerry to Vietnam to battle childhood malnutrition. Upon his arrival, the Vietnamese government told Jerry that he had six months to demonstrate a reduction in malnutrition, or his visa would not be extended. The government also provided him with documentation showing that traditional supplemental feeding programs had been tried but failed to provide any long-term benefits. Jerry had to come up with a unique approach that was both preventative and therapeutic, utilizing the resources available within the community. He chose a method called positive deviance. The basic concept was to identify well-nourished children from very poor families, the positive deviants, and determine what these families were doing differently. By getting other people in the community to adopt the practices that these families employed, Jerry believed he would be able to combat malnutrition with solutions that already existed in the community."

"Jerry and his team identified a site to pilot the positive deviance approach. They targeted four villages just south of Hanoi that had an extremely high rate of malnutrition. Then, they identified six of the poorest families with well-nourished children from each of the four villages. Teams were established to visit these homes at mealtime to observe hygiene, food prep, and cooking methods. What the teams discovered was that, in these homes, the parents were collecting tiny shrimps, crabs, or snails while working in the rice paddies and were adding them to the children's rice. In addition, these families were adding sweet potato greens to the rice. Sweet potato greens were free and available in abundance in the area. Jerry then had these families share this information with the other members of the village and requested that all families adopt these practices. By the end of their six-month deadline, these villages experienced forty-percent rehabilitation. In addition, another twenty percent of children moved from severely malnourished to moderate levels of malnutrition. Jerry's visa was extended."

"That's a great story, but what does it have to do with our plan?" interrupted Joe.

"Actually, there are several things that relate to our plan, but first let me finish," replied Donna as she continued her story. "I conducted some additional research because I wanted to know if this was just a flash in the pan or if the results were sustained. I found that the program was incredibly successful, with the most remarkable results coming from an independent follow-up study conducted ten years after Jerry had left

Vietnam. The Harvard School of Public Health did the study. It was conducted at the four original villages. What they found was that the children who were not yet born when Jerry left the village were at the same nutritional level as their older siblings. This demonstrates that the outcomes were sustained. The dietary changes that were established became a permanent part of the community culture."

"Okay," said Joe. "I'm still not grasping the relevance. I mean it's a great story with impressive results, but you're not suggesting that we abandon Lean and go with this positive deviance approach, are you?"

"No, not at all. However, the story does provide evidence that we are on the right track. First of all, the positive deviance or PD approach employed bottom-up implementation. The solution to malnutrition already existed in the community, but for whatever reason, other families failed to adopt the practices, even though the practices would provide a healthy diet for their children. This demonstrates the importance of listening to people, not only because they might provide a solution but also because we may need their cooperation as we move forward with a plan. If we fail to listen to them early on, they may feel that we don't believe they have anything of value to contribute. Also, PD allowed these people to solve this formidable problem utilizing resources that already existed in the villages. Lastly, and Joe, you'll like this. The solution did not require any initial outlay of finances, nor did it require periodic funding to sustain the results. Instead, it utilized resources that were readily available in the community."

"So what you're saying is that the remedies to our troubles lie within these very walls," said Nick. "We don't need to go outside looking for solutions or to hire consultants to fix our processes."

"That's one thing I'm saying. There is a quote from Jerry that says, 'The traditional model for organizational change doesn't work. It never has. You can't bring permanent solutions in from the outside.' In order for any change to be sustainable, it must come from the bottom up. Our experience with Janice established that the staff was reluctant to adopt changes recommended by an outsider who lacks familiarity with the processes. I believe that bottom-up implementation is a critical component to successful implementation."

"I also liked the 'listening' portion of the story. It falls into alignment with what I believe is a supporting element for our plan. I labeled it respect for people. I'll talk about it in more detail when it's my turn," added Nick. "Does anybody else have anything they'd like to share?"

Ron raised his hand. "I found some information about the importance of training. What I found involved a joint venture between Toyota and General Motors. I won't go into a lot of details. I'll get right to the point. The plan was to reopen a GM manufacturing plant in Freemont, California and build both Toyota and GM vehicles. The joint venture was named NUMMI, an acronym for New United Motor Manufacturing Incorporated. NUMMI was contacted by the United Auto Workers Union, who informed them that if they planned to reopen the plant, they would have to hire back the work force who had lost their jobs when the plant closed. Somewhat amusingly, the union described these people as 'the worst work force in the automobile industry in the United States.' There were stories of people drinking on the job or having sex in the plant, absenteeism was rampant, and quality was pretty much nonexistent. There were even stories of petty acts of sabotage, such as workers putting soda bottles in door panels to cause unidentifiable rattling. Undaunted, Toyota agreed to rehire these people. As they neared the time to begin production, GM wanted to immediately start implementing change by conducting *kaizen* events that they had heard so much about. However, Toyota insisted that the work force first undergo training in Lean principles. They conducted mostly classroom training, but some individuals were sent to Japan to work side by side with the Japanese workers on the assembly line at the Toyota plant. As a result of their training, the workers understood and applied the tools and principles of Lean on the production floor at the NUMMI plant. Almost immediately, the quality of cars leaving the NUMMI plant rivaled the quality of cars made by Toyota in Japan. They took a work force considered by their own union to be the worst work force in the automotive industry and, through training, turned them into a team who was as good as the best in the automotive industry. This ties in well with Donna's story because we can only have bottom-up implementation if the staff understands the tools and concepts. We need to provide proper training. I know we spoke about training on Friday, but I think this story validates the need."

Dr. Albert added, "I agree. Studies have demonstrated that training is the single most critical element relative to culture change."

Nick turned to Donna and asked if she had any luck finding someone to conduct the training.

"Not yet. I did find a couple of conferences. There are some speakers who I think might be potential candidates."

"Good! Betty, can you get the information from Donna and make arrangements for her to attend these conferences and to speak to these possible candidates?"

"I already have her registered for the conference, and I'm in the process of making travel arrangements," replied Betty. Nick smiled and shook his head, amazed that Betty always seemed to be one step ahead of him.

"Well, we're running out of time, but I have something I want to go over." Nick removed copies of the sketch he did of the house of Lean and passed them around. He explained that the three key elements of Lean: standard work, user-friendliness, and unobstructed throughput were critical to building a strong foundation. He then explained the three supporting elements, *jidoka*, *kaizen*, and respect for people, and his reasoning for choosing them. "I believe that these elements in conjunction with a strong foundation will support our plan. Now, we just need something to tie it all together."

Megan asked, "What about flow?"

"What about it?" asked Nick.

"From what I've been reading, it seems to me that the ultimate goal is to create flow. The reason I focused on flow was because I remembered Donna mentioning it at our first meeting. I have been struggling with this idea of flow since I heard her say the word. I understand how to create flow in a manufacturing environment. What I was having a difficulty with was creating flow in a healthcare environment. We have no control over our volumes. We have emergencies almost every day, and the support functions have conflicting priorities. I didn't want to be the voice of doom, so I kept this concern to myself until I could learn more. There is a concept in Lean called *heijunka*. What the word means is leveling or smoothing the production process. It is complex and utilizes many Lean tools and concepts that I don't thoroughly understand, such as takt time, pull systems, standard work in process, mixed-model production, and *kanbans*, just to name a few. Personally, I don't believe that we can create flow for all our processes all the time. The more I thought about it, the more it confirmed my belief. We can't have continuous flow one hundred percent of the time. However, perhaps we can have it eighty percent of the time. If we could accomplish that, we would be a million times better off than we are now." She noticed Joe giving her a skeptical look. She responded before he could say anything. "I know. A million times is an exaggeration. The point I'm making is that we would be much better off than we are now. Anyway, I think that this *heijunka* concept should also be a supporting element."

Donna agreed with Megan, adding, "Lean is about creating flow, and I think that Megan has hit the nail on the head. We can't abandon Lean because it's not going to work a hundred percent of the time. The improvement methodology that will work all the time, under all conditions, doesn't exist."

Nick took out his pen and added the fourth supporting element, labeled it *heijunka*, and requested that everyone else do the same. "Now, we need something that ties it all together. Any suggestions?"

Elizabeth said, "In order to get the different components of a system to operate efficiently and effectively, there must be a shared objective. The only possible shared objective for a hospital is a total focus on the care and safety of the patient. What ties it all together is the patient."

"Excellent point. However, I don't believe the focus is specific to the patients themselves. I believe it's how we process the patient or the care delivery system. They have a name for this in Lean," said Donna as she flipped through her handout. "Yes, here it is. They refer to it as the value stream. The definition in the handout is *the sequence of activities required to bring a product from order receipt through to delivery of the finished product to the hands of the customer.* For our purposes, we can define it as everything that happens to a patient from the time he or she presents to the time he or she is discharged. We can call it a value stream focus."

"Great, I like it," exclaimed Nick. "Now, how about the roof? How do we top this off? Many of the houses of Lean that I saw on the Internet labeled it continuous improvement. I don't agree with that because *kaizen* is continuous improvement, and we have it listed as a supporting element. Others had labels like value, delivery, pursuit of perfection, and vision."

"I think the pursuit of perfection sounds good," said Joe.

"I did, too," said Nick. "But when you think about it, the pursuit of perfection is continuous improvement."

"That's true," responded Joe.

Nick continued, "Several houses had the label TPS, which is an acronym for the Toyota Production System. What that says to me is that the roof should be our final goal. In our case, the final goal is to be a Lean enterprise." Nick got up and drew the house of Lean on the flip chart.

```
                    /\
                   /  \
                  /    \
                 /      \
                /        \
               /  Lean    \
              /  enterprise \
             /_____\
            | Value stream focus |
            |_____|
            | |    | |    | |    | |
            | |    | |    | |    | |
         J  | | K  | | R  | | H  | |
         i  | | a  | | e  | | e  | |
         d  | | i  | | s  | | i  | |
         o  | | z  | | p  | | j  | |
         k  | | e  | | e  | | u  | |
         a  | | n  | | c  | | n  | |
            | |    | | t  | | k  | |
            | |    | | f  | | a  | |
            | |    | | o  | |    | |
            | |    | | r  | |    | |
            | |    | |    | |    | |
            | |    | | p  | |    | |
            | |    | | e  | |    | |
            | |    | | o  | |    | |
            | |    | | p  | |    | |
            | |    | | l  | |    | |
            | |    | | e  | |    | |
   _____|_|____|_|____|_|____|_|_____
  | Standard work, user-friendliness, and unobstructed throughput |
  |_____|
```

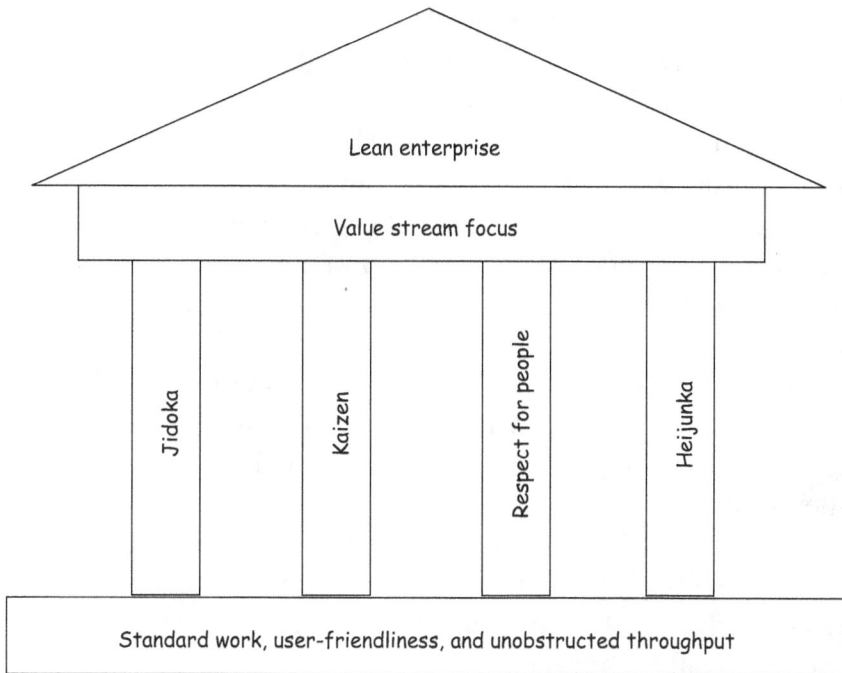

When he finished, he stepped back to get a better look and said, "That's better! It's not too complex. It will need some explanation, but I think we have it. Any comments or suggestions?" When no one responded, Nick ended the meeting and again thanked everyone for all the time and effort they'd expended.

After the meeting, Nick sat down at his desk to get some work done. He heard a knock on the opened office door. When he looked up, he saw Asha standing in the doorway with Cora and Tammy. Nick stood and greeted them and asked that they have a seat at the conference table. He wasn't quite sure how to begin and decided to ask them how they liked the new process.

"I don't really like it," responded Cora. "I think the way we were doing it before was just fine. I don't understand why we have to change."

"How about you, Tammy, what do you think?"

"I kind of like it. I don't really like sitting around waiting. I'm a traveling tech, so the sooner I get done here, the sooner I can head out for my next job."

Nick turned to Cora and said, "Let me explain why we need to change. Dr. Snyder is spending too much time here at the hospital doing these tests. Consequently, she can't see patients in her office for morning appointments. She told me she was going to start doing the tests in her office if we didn't make some changes."

"Well, why is it always about what the doctors want? They never accommodate us when we need something. They just go around making demands, and everyone has to do what they want."

"The doctors bring in the money, Cora. We can't generate any revenue on our own. Everything we do requires the doctor's orders. Also, in reality, they can and have been very accommodating in the past."

"Okay, but I still don't like the new process. It's different. I'm not used to working this way. I think I might make an error because I'm rushed, and that wouldn't be a good thing." The tone of Cora's last statement could have easily been misinterpreted as a threat.

Nick knew that Cora didn't mean this as a threat but rather as a form of resistance to change. He understood that change was difficult because it meant doing things differently. Doing things differently, in turn, required leaving one's comfort zone. He didn't want to attempt to force Cora out of her comfort zone. He knew he had to come up with some way to make her want to change. He scanned his memory banks and hit on something he thought might work. "Cora," he said. "If you would be willing to give this new process a serious effort, say, for three weeks, I'll make you a promise. At the end of the three weeks, if you still don't like the process, I will make any changes you suggest or change it back to the way it was before."

Asha's jaw almost hit the floor. "Nick, I don't think…"

Nick cut her off and looked at Cora for a response. "That sounds fair. Three weeks, I'll mark my calendar."

"Okay, then I think we're done here," said Nick, as he motioned for Asha to stay.

Cora and Tammy left the office, and Nick sat at the conference table with Asha. "I know you're confused Asha, but I am conducting a little experiment. Have you ever heard of Dr. Maxwell Maltz?"

Asha shook her head and asked, "Does he work here?"

"No," replied Nick with a smile. "He was a plastic surgeon in the nineteen-fifties. He noticed a pattern among his patients. After he performed surgery, there would be an adjustment period for his patients to adapt to the change. He discovered that it would take almost exactly twenty-one days for a patient who, let's say, had a nose job to get used to his or her new face. He began to study the adjustment periods for other behaviors and found that it took approximately twenty-one days to develop a new habit. Cora doesn't like the new process, not because it doesn't work but because it requires her to do things differently from the way she is used to doing them. She is being forced out of her comfort zone, and she doesn't like it. It's uncomfortable. I'm betting that if she does it consistently for twenty-one days, she will get used to the changes, it will feel comfortable, and she will agree to follow the new standard work."

"I hope you're right. In the meantime, I can't spend my mornings down there for the next three weeks, making sure they follow the new process."

"You shouldn't have to. If they're not following the new standard work, I'm sure Dr. Snyder will let us know."

"Yes, we can count on that."

"This doesn't mean you are out of the loop. Make sure you don't ignore them. Stop by and ask how things are going. Give them some praise, but only if it is authentic. Don't make up accolades just to sound positive. If the compliments are contrived, they'll see right through them. Let's keep our fingers crossed."

He escorted her out of his office and continued on with his day.

Chapter 11

Creating the Plan

Donna wasn't present for the Tuesday morning crisis meeting. She was on her way to a conference in San Diego, in hopes of finding someone to conduct Lean training. Everyone else was present, and Nick began the meeting. "I want to start this morning by once again thanking all of you for your help. We've collected a lot of information, identified a methodology, discussed implementation, and identified pitfalls. We're getting very close to Friday's presentation. I'd like to discuss how to best put all this information into an understandable format. I'm thinking I'd like to open with Joe's 'Reactive Cycle for Dealing with Financial Instability.' I will explain how our method for dealing with the hospital's financial situation has had a negative effect on quality. We will need some hard numbers here, Joe. I know that you have compiled some very useful data, but anything else you can get before Friday will be helpful. I don't want to talk in general terms or use national averages. I know the board members will be asking for specific examples here at the hospital. Next, I'll explain how layoffs and budget cuts have created an environment where people are overwhelmed and overburdened, which, in turn, has led to an increase in errors. I will use Megan's graphs to confirm this information."

Megan interrupted him saying, "Nick, it's extremely important that the board understand that my staff is working very hard and that they are dealing with very real problems, but that the system that's in place does not support them. I don't want it to sound like they're the reason for the increase in errors."

Ron added, "Not just your staff, the entire staff. Granted, the nurses are picking up many extra duties, but it's because my departments are so short staffed. The people who are left are working extremely hard trying to keep up. It's just not possible."

"Megan, I know this is weighing heavy on your mind. I promise you that I will make it crystal clear that the staff has gone above and beyond." Nick then looked at Ron and added, "The entire staff!"

Nick then turned his attention back to the presentation. "I believe that with Joe's numbers and Megan's graph, we can make our case for the need to focus on improving quality. I'm looking for help on how to introduce our decision to adopt Lean as our methodology."

"I think we should follow up the reactive cycle with the importance of culture change and systems thinking," responded Elizabeth.

"Boy, that's a surprise," responded Nick with a smile to let Elizabeth know he was joking. "Actually, I agree. I think that it's important for the board members to understand that the culture and the system necessary to improve do not exist at the present time. I believe that to get this point across, we explain the present culture and system. We have a culture that does not put the patient first and a system that is departmentally focused."

"I think that's all you need to say. If they want examples, we can provide them," responded Elizabeth.

"Should we talk about how we plan to change the culture and create a system?" asked Ron. "Maybe we should talk about results, behaviors, beliefs, and experiences."

"I don't think so," said Nick. "I don't want to lose their attention. If we start to go into detail, we may lose them. I want to explain the plan, not the rationale or the implementation of the plan. If they ask why this plan is going to work where others have failed, we can then talk about the results progression. I think at this point, as perilous as it might be, we're going to have to introduce Lean."

"Be prepared. You'll probably get a similar reaction to the one that Donna got when she suggested Lean to us," said Joe. "You weren't here when Janice was contracted to implement Lean, but the board members were. They're going to assume that you don't have prior experience with Lean, and they may shut you down."

"That's good advice, Joe! Maybe I should begin by explaining why it failed in the past."

"I disagree," said Elizabeth. "As you mentioned earlier, we don't want to focus on implementation or rationale. Tell them the plan, and then answer their questions. It will demonstrate that you've done your homework and you are confident that this will work."

"So, are you suggesting that I just say that we've decided to adopt Lean as our plan for improving financial stability?"

"Yes, I am!"

"No way," exclaimed Joe. "That would be suicide. I think it would be better to talk about eliminating wasteful… No wait, I wouldn't even say wasteful. Let's see. Maybe you should say that the plan is to design a system where what is supposed to happen, does happen."

Megan added, "When it's supposed to happen, in the order it's supposed to happen."

"Right!" said Joe. "Allowing our patients to receive high-quality care, without delays or errors."

"That's not bad," said Nick. "Then, I can introduce Lean as the methodology for accomplishing these objectives."

"I still think you need to stay away from the word Lean until the very end," insisted Joe. "I would explain that we will develop standard work, make our processes user-friendly, and eliminate obstructions to flow. Then, I would add that we are going to make our problems obvious, continuously improve, encourage staff involvement, and create patient flow. Finally, you can say we plan to do this across the entire spectrum of services offered at the hospital. This might be a good time to mention that whether we operate as a system or not does not change the fact that a hospital is a system. Every department in the hospital either provides or receives a service from other departments."

"I like it, Joe! You've encapsulated the entire house of Lean into a few sentences. However, I would leave out the last part about the system and hold it for answering questions."

Ron asked, "When are we going to talk about bringing operations up to speed?"

"I think it would be appropriate at this point," replied Nick. "We are going to need approval for a few things to make this work. We need to rehire eighteen FTEs and hire someone to conduct training. There will be capital costs associated with improvements, et cetera. I liked what Donna said about the cost of poor quality being greater than the cost of quality." He looked over at Betty and asked if she captured her statement in the minutes.

"Yes I did," replied Betty as she began to shuffle through her notes. "I thought it might be important. She said, 'There are four categories of quality costs. There are prevention cost, inspection cost, the cost of internal failures, and the cost of external failures. The first two are the costs of quality. The last two are the costs of poor quality. It is a universal misconception that the cost of quality is greater than the cost of poor quality. Consequently, errors are often shrugged off as just coming with the territory.'"

"That's perfect!" exclaimed Joe as he pulled up his data on his tablet. "Now, you can compare the cost of medical errors caused by overburdened staff, such as hospital-associated infections (HAIs), with the cost of restaffing operations. The

HAIs cost one million, eight hundred and thirty-eight thousand, one hundred dollars. Our original estimate for restaffing operations was a little low. I came up with a more accurate number. For the eighteen FTEs, I estimated approximately seven hundred and sixty-three thousand dollars for the first year. That includes benefits and administrative costs involved in the hiring process. It is less than half the cost of HAIs. Also, keep in mind that HAIs are not the only cost of poor quality."

"This sounds good," said Nick. "I'll start putting the presentation together. Between now and Friday, I'd like to have Ron, Megan, and Joe review the handout and try to implement a Lean tool. I think it would be great if I can give real-life examples of the application of Lean tools to the board. I'd like each of you to experiment with a different tool, so let's decide who will do what. Okay, we have 5S, mistake proofing, quick changeover, *kanban*, and visual controls. Let's start with these."

"I'll take quick changeover," said Ron.

"I'll take mistake proofing. It seems logical," added Megan.

Joe said, "Well that leaves 5S, *kanban*, and visual controls. What's a *kanban*?"

"It's an inventory control system for replenishing products used in production. It is also used to maintain supply levels," answered Nick.

"Okay, I'll do that."

"Great! Okay, let's call it a day. This has been another productive meeting. Oh, one more thing. When you implement these tools, be certain to follow the three rules we established for the status boards. Focus on the process and low cost, and stay within the department's area of influence. Let's skip tomorrow's meeting so you can focus on these implementations. We'll get back together on Thursday and finalize the presentation."

The meeting ended, and Nick sat at his desk very satisfied with the effort everyone had put in. He turned on his computer and began organizing the information for Friday's presentation.

Chapter 12

Some Results

Wednesday, Nick spent all his free time preparing for the presentation. On Thursday morning, he felt pretty comfortable with the finished product and brought it out to Betty. "Could you please create some slides that I can use for this presentation? I think we may want to provide handouts, also. I would just print the slides for a handout. Don't go to a lot of trouble. Oh, one more thing. Don't try to dress it up too much. A few graphics might be useful but nothing that will distract from the information I'm presenting."

"I'll take care of it," replied Betty. "Nick, I just want to say that I think you've nailed it. This plan seems pretty solid. You covered all the bases, and I'm praying that it gets approved."

"Thanks Betty. That means a lot. What time is today's crisis meeting?"

"I scheduled it for the end of the day, just in case you need extra time. So it starts at two."

"Betty, you think of everything. Thanks again." With that, Nick went back to his office.

At one-thirty, he was surprised to see Donna come into his office. "I thought you were at a conference in San Diego," he said. "I was. I think I've found the perfect person to conduct the training. We had dinner together last night, and I explained what we wanted and how we planned on proceeding. He was surprised and said, 'You know, I've been trying to get people to implement correctly for years, but they always want to go right into implementation.' He was very interested, and he can't wait to start. Oh, and he is reasonably priced."

"When can he start?"

"Well, I wasn't sure what to tell him, since it all hinges on Friday's meeting, but I told him I would be in touch."

"Great! Are you coming to the crisis meeting, or are you too wiped out from the trip?"

"I wouldn't miss it for the world. A little bird told me that you gave Ron, Joe, and Megan assignments. They're actually implementing Lean tools?"

"Yes, it should be interesting. See you in half an hour."

At two o'clock, everyone was seated around the conference table, and Ron, Joe, and Megan all had smiles on their faces. "Okay, I'm not sure what the smiles are about, but I'm anxious to find out. First, you probably noticed that Donna is back. She found a consultant to do the training. I'll let her tell you about it."

Donna told everyone about her meeting in more detail and indicated that she felt really good about the consultant and was looking forward to having everyone meet him. She explained that she told the consultant he would have to come in and meet with the leadership team prior to an actual engagement, and he was fine with that.

Nick took over again, "Okay, before the three of you burst out of your skin, who wants to go first?"

Ron raised his hand. "After Tuesday's meeting, I reviewed the handout section on quick changeover. It is actually referred to in Lean as SMED, which is an acronym for single-minute exchange of die. An industrial engineer named Shigeo Shingo developed this method for changing over dies in manufacturing plants. What he meant by single minute was less than ten minutes, or single digits of minutes. The method sorts the operations into three categories. An operation conducted during changeover is either internal, meaning the machine is not running, or external, meaning operations conducted when the machine is running. The final category is waste, or operations that are not necessary. Anyway, I was having a difficult time deciding on a process when I ran into Asha. She was so impressed with the nuclear stress test results that she volunteered her department. I explained the SMED concept to her, and she suggested looking at CT scans." Ron then passed out a sheet of paper. The process steps were listed on the paper Ron passed out:

1. CT ends on previous patient, and the machine is stopped.
2. Remove IV from the patient.
3. Patient removed from table.
4. Patient is brought out of the CT scan room.
5. The next patient is brought into the CT scan room.
6. Ascertain patient ID.
7. Explain procedure to the patient.
8. Physician's orders are verified.
9. IV is started on the patient.
10. Patient is placed on table.
11. CT scanner is turned on, and scan is started.

"What we noticed was that all of the steps were being conducted as internal operations, or when the scanner was off. So, we discussed how we could make them external operations. We set up a small prep room with a computer, and a school desk for starting IVs, and we stocked it with supplies. Now, many of the operations are conducted externally, and the new process is shown on the next page."

1. CT ends on previous patient, and the machine is stopped.
2. Patient removed from table.
3. Patient is brought out of the CT scan room.
4. The next patient is brought into the CT scan room.
5. Patient is placed on table.
6. CT scanner is turned on, and scan is started.

"Asha is so excited she can't wait to start implementing more Lean tools. She said that she believed she could double the number of CT scans she can do in a day, which will significantly reduce her backlog. This simple change will enhance revenue, maximize the utilization of the CT scanner, and increase patient satisfaction."

"Impressive!" said Nick.

"I stuck to the rules, but there is a cost. The manufacturer of the scanner informed us that we would have to upgrade to a high-performance x-ray tube. However, the return on investment will be relatively short."

"I can see why you were so excited. Okay Megan, your turn."

"I did mistake proofing or what the Japanese call *poka-yoke*. We had a mistake in the ED earlier this week. A nurse mistakenly administered epinephrine IV. The nurse and I used a mistake-proofing worksheet, from the back of Janice's handout, to identify the root cause. What we discovered was that the epinephrine stored in the pyxis is single-use ampules. So, to draw up the epinephrine, she had used an IM syringe with a filter straw. She also drew a syringe of Solu-Medrol, also in an IM syringe. Because it was an emergency situation and she was in a rush, she ran to the patient's bedside, administered the Solu-Medrol, and immediately followed it up with the epinephrine. She realized her mistake immediately and took appropriate action. I went to the pharmacy and asked why they stocked the epinephrine in ampules instead of vials, and they told me that epinephrine is not available in single-use vials. So to prevent wasting medication, they stocked ampules. I did some research with the pharmacist and found that the ampule costs forty-nine cents. A multiuse vial costs a dollar ninety-seven. However, the filter straw costs ninety-two cents. We subtracted the cost of the ampule and filter straw from the cost of the vial and came up with fifty-six cents. The pharmacy agreed to make a prepackaged epi allergy kit and stock it in the pyxis. The kit includes a multidose vial, a TB syringe, and an alcohol wipe, all neatly packaged in a ziplock bag with a label."

"Nice, I like this," said Nick. "Okay Joe, you're up."

"I had *kanban*. I was struggling with this in my area, so I set up a supply *kanban*. I just inserted a card at the replenishment point. When, whatever the supply happens to be, say, sticky notes, is removed, the card is dropped in a bin on the supply room door. Each day, Sally, the administrative secretary, picks up the cards and sends them to purchasing. Purchasing replenishes the supplies, and the card is reinserted at the replenishment point. It's pretty sweet. Sally doesn't have to inventory the supplies or make out requisitions. It worked so well that when I showed it to Megan, she wanted to try it on one of the nursing units. We used a different system, which I'd like to take credit for, but it was one of the nurses' idea. Instead of using cards, we implemented a double bin system. There are two bins for each part number. Each bin had a full par level to start. We did have to implement standard work, but it's pretty simple. The standard work says you can only take supplies from the top bin. When the top bin is empty, they switch it with the bottom bin. The empty bottom bin is the signal to replenish the supplies. The par levels were calculated using the daily usage, the order size, and the response time, and we added a buffer based on fluctuations in use or erratic delivery cycles. Obtaining supplies is now user-friendly. Other benefits are that there are fewer supplies kept on hand just in case, and since the supplies get rotated, we won't have to throw any away due to age-related deterioration. The nurses love it."

Megan added, "I've already received requests from other units to do the same thing."

"So, by involving the nurse, it sounds as though the news spread pretty quickly," stated Nick. "Also, we're more likely to sustain the gains, and we changed their experiences. This is very good."

"I have to say, I'm amazed," said Donna. "I wasn't sure what to expect given the reaction I received when I brought up the idea of Lean, but it looks like we have buy-in among senior leadership."

"I finished my presentation this morning, and Betty is organizing it for me and creating some slides and handouts," said Nick. "I can't thank all of you enough. I really appreciate the way everyone contributed. If we don't get approval, I'd like you all to come work for me at my new job."

Everyone laughed nervously.

"Seriously though, this has been an exciting two weeks, and I'm pretty confident we'll get the approval."

Elizabeth said, "I think I speak for everyone when I say, it's been a pleasure and that we want to be at the meeting with you to show our support for the plan."

"That's really not necessary."

"We know it's not necessary. We want to be there."

"Yeah," said Joe. "You think we did all this work and we're going to let you hog all the credit?"

"Well that was my plan," said Nick, jokingly. "Seriously, I think it would be great to have all of you there with me."

Chapter 13

Follow-Up Board Meeting

On Friday evening, Nick pulled into the hospital parking lot for the board meeting. The air was crisp and clear, the exact opposite of when he arrived for his last board meeting. He had a bit of a spring in his step as he walked into the hospital. When he entered the boardroom, all the board members were present, and Dr. Richardson said, "Oh good, you're here. Why don't you get yourself set up so we can start?" As he walked to the front of the room, Nick noticed Ray Driscoll rocking back and forth in his chair, with his arms folded across his chest and a malevolent smile on his face. Nick acknowledged him with a slight nod, which was not returned. As he was getting ready, his team walked in together and took seats in front of the room with Nick. Ray's smile vanished and was replaced by a confused expression. Then, Nick passed around the handouts and signaled to Dr. Richardson that he was ready.

"Okay, as you all know, we are here tonight to evaluate Nick's plan for dealing with the hospital's financial crisis and either approve or reject it. I think it would be best if we hear the plan in its entirety without interruption. So if you have questions, jot them down, and we will have a Q&A session when Nick is finished." He looked at Nick and gave him a nod to proceed.

Nick began by thanking everyone for allowing him the two weeks extension to prepare and then proceeded with his presentation.

"Before I begin, I want to make one thing perfectly clear. The only person to blame for the current financial situation here at the hospital is standing before you. The people who work here are dedicated, competent, and compassionate people. They have gone the extra mile to do whatever is necessary to provide the best possible care for their patients. They do this without complaint or resentment. I hold each and every one of them in the highest esteem, and they are the only reason our doors are still open." He looked over at Megan who gave him a nod and a smile.

"We have identified the cost of poor quality as the major contributor to our financial dilemma. Joe has compiled some data to support this premise, which you will see on the first page of your handout." Nick pulled up the first slide of his presentation, which displayed Joe's numbers. "Please note that his data are associated exclusively with hospital-associated infections or HAIs. This is not the total cost of poor quality."

Last Fiscal Year				
4995 Admissions Resulted in 201 Hospital-Associated Infections				
PERCENTAGE	HAI	AVG COST	NUMBER	COST
30%	CAUTI	$1158	60	$69,827
20%	SSI	$20,712	40	$832,622
10%	VAP	$11,476	20	$230,667
10%	CLABSI	$19,049	20	$382,885
30%	OTHER	$7000	60	$422,100
Total Cost: $1,838,101				

"We also have data that show that the methods we have employed in the past to deal with financial instability have led to a decline in quality." Nick advanced his presentation to the next slide, which showed Megan's scatter diagram displaying the positive correlation between layoffs and the increase in errors.

SCATTER DIAGRAM DISPLAYING THE RELATIONSHIP BETWEEN LAYOFFS AND ERRORS

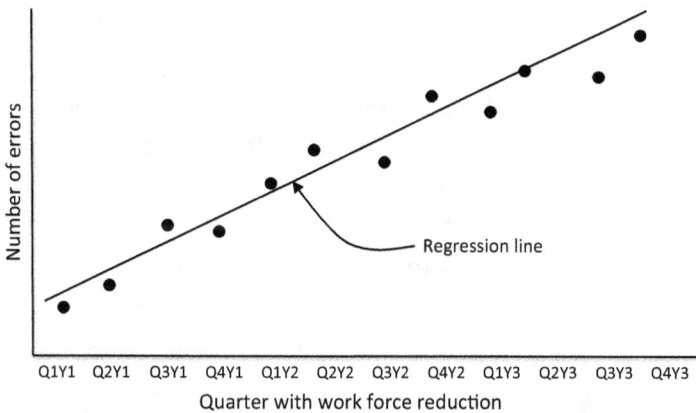

"As you can see from this diagram, the layoffs began one year prior to my accepting the CEO position and have occurred every year since then. Correspondingly, the number of errors has increased."

Nick then pulled up a slide showing the reactive cycle for dealing with financial instability. He explained how financial instability has led to bad decisions leading to poor quality, which, in turn, is worsening the hospital's financial situation.

"Layoffs, budget cuts, program cancellations, and other bad decisions we have employed in the past inhibit growth and have evoked a work force that is overworked, overburdened, and overwhelmed. This, in turn, has ushered in a culture in which the patient is no longer our priority. The present culture within the hospital views errors as something that comes with the territory. This is the first thing we need to change. The patient must be our number one priority. Our patients are the reason why we are here. Without them, there is no reason for this hospital to exist. Therefore, it is imperative that our plan be centered on doing what is best for the patient.

"Of equal importance is the necessity of creating a system. Currently, we operate as departmentally focused silos that do what is best for the department as opposed to doing what is best for the patient. Silos lead to mistrust, rivalry, increased patient wait times, finger-pointing, communication breakdowns, errors, and waste. It is critical that we operate as a system in which everyone is working together for the good of the patient.

"In order to accomplish these two objectives, a long-term commitment to change is required. Our processes are not standardized allowing errors to progress unnoticed. They are not user-friendly necessitating waiting and searching, which robs the staff of precious time and encourages the implementation of work-arounds and stopgap measures. Finally, our processes are plagued with obstructions to flow resulting in extensive patient wait times, delays in care, and extremely low patient satisfaction scores.

"Our plan requires, first and foremost, that we make problems obvious. We can't fix what we're not aware of. By standardizing our processes, any problems will become easily discernable. Once the problems are identified, we will commence with immediate problem resolution and follow up with root cause analysis to formulate countermeasures to prevent the error from recurring.

"In addition, the plan will instill a philosophy of continuous improvement. This plan requires that every employee be attentive to opportunities for improvement. Accordingly, leadership and management must support and respond to these opportunities, recognizing that our staff members are the authorities relative to their processes. Also, the plan will address obstructions to flow by balancing our processes, adjusting staffing levels, and refining the distribution of the workload. These four things, making problems obvious, continuous improvement, bottom-up implementation, and flow, will be incorporated throughout the organization, thereby establishing the building blocks necessary for systems thinking." With this, Nick concluded his presentation and asked for questions.

Ray Driscoll had the first question. "Very good presentation," he said insincerely. "How exactly do you plan to accomplish all this?"

"Very good question," responded Nick, mildly mimicking Ray's insincerity. "First of all, the plan requires proper implementation. Implementation has three components. First, we must educate the staff in the principles we wish to incorporate. Second involves bottom-up implementation. The third involves systems thinking."

"Could you be more specific? What are these principles you plan on incorporating?"

"Well, first is our focus on quality. In order to obtain the desired results, we must change behaviors. Because we are so short staffed, the remaining staff is required to do more. They are taking on surplus duties and accepting additional responsibilities. This circumstance has spawned behaviors that support doing what is easy rather than what is best for the patient. This behavior is the result of the belief that the organization values money over patient care and safety. In turn, these beliefs are confirmed because of what the staff has experienced. Work force reductions, budget cuts, and cost-cutting measures such as purchasing low-cost, inferior supplies have only reinforced these beliefs. This plan was established on the premise that we must first change experiences before we can change behaviors."

Susan asked, "How will this plan change these experiences?"

"Excellent question!" responded Nick. "There are several factors involved in changing experiences. What it boils down to, however, is demonstrating respect for the work force. To accomplish this, we will incorporate what we have decided to call status boards. These boards will allow the staff to alert management to problems and issues that need attention without fear that the issue will be ignored. Rules have been established for the use of these boards to prevent finger-pointing and unrealistic requests."

"I can imagine that there will be a plethora of issues going up on these status boards," said Ray using finger quotes to emphasize the term status boards. "Who exactly is going to have the responsibility for addressing all of these issues?"

"Part of the plan is to educate all of our directors and managers, providing them with the necessary tools and knowledge to deal with these issues. They will work closely with the staff to formulate and implement solutions." Rather than affording Ray the opportunity for more questions, Nick decided to let the cat out of the bag. "The methodology we will be employing was derived from the Toyota Production System and is referred to as Lean."

Jim Donahue, always a supporter of Nick, calmly asked, "Nick, are you aware of the fact that we attempted to implement Lean in the past, and it was, shall I say, less than successful?"

"Yes, Jim, I am. As a matter of fact, when Donna first suggested the idea of implementing Lean, we rejected it. However, she persisted, and the more we studied and experimented with the methodology, the more convinced we became that it was just what we needed."

"Wait a minute!" said Ray. "We hired a professional consultant to come to the organization and implement Lean. Are you suggesting that you know more about the methodology than she does?"

"No, Ray. She was very knowledgeable and had years of experience, but her implementation method is what led to failure. People were not familiar with the tools, the terms, or the Japanese words she used. She attempted to drive people from their comfort zone with demands and threats. She instituted process changes without first understanding the complexities of the processes. Essentially, she imposed changes to our processes that either did not work or were not sustainable."

Dr. Richardson, in an attempt to get the meeting under control, asked, "Nick, please explain this in more detail, what you're going to do and how you plan on doing it."

"Before I can do that, I must first explain a few things. First of all, we need our improvements to be sustainable. If they are not sustainable, all of our time, effort, and money will be for naught. Sustainability can only be achieved if we have buy-in from the staff. They must understand the tools and concepts associated with the methodology. In addition, changes must come from the bottom up. The people who best understand the processes and those who must live with the changes must be the ones to improve the processes."

"That sounds a lot like empowerment!" exclaimed Ray.

"It is empowerment," replied Nick, "with two big differences. First, changes will be implemented with the support and guidance of management. And, second, rules have been established to prevent finger-pointing.

"As I was saying," continued Nick, "the improvements must be sustainable, which means changing the culture. We will accomplish this by changing people's experiences rather than attempting to change behaviors. The status boards will be the vehicles for accomplishing this. Second, we must change the system. This can only be accomplished by eliminating silos. To achieve systems thinking, we will provide the departments with strategically focused objectives rather than departmental goals."

"You plan to accomplish this using Lean concepts?" asked Ray. "You're asking us to give approval to a methodology that has already failed, with no proof that it is going to be any different going forward."

"Actually, we have successfully implemented Lean tools here at the hospital." Nick told them about the application of one-piece flow in the nuclear stress test. He then had Ron, Joe, and Megan convey their experiences on implementing the quick changeover, *kanbans*, and mistake proofing. When they were finished, Nick summarized the benefits of the implementation of the four Lean concepts.

"This is extraordinary!" stated Susan. "However, where will you find the time to manage process improvement initiatives? Your job is to run the organization, not to conduct improvement events."

"That's the beauty of this plan, Susan. The staff will identify the issues and work with management to develop and implement changes. Management will receive comprehensive training in Lean tools allowing them to provide the necessary guidance to their staff. Senior leadership's role will be to address any barriers encountered during the implementation phase."

Dr. Richardson said, "I would imagine that there will be many barriers, considering that you, yourself, stated that 'we work in departmentally focused silos.'"

"We did anticipate that as a possible problem. To address that possibility, rule number three states 'no crossing departmental boundaries.'" Nick then expounded on all the other benefits of this rule.

Dr. Richardson looked up at the ceiling and rubbed his chin. After a few seconds, he looked at Nick and said, "Let me see if I have this right. You will begin by providing comprehensive training in Lean tools and concepts for directors and managers. How about the staff?"

"The staff will receive an initial overview and will then receive additional training in small increments. We didn't feel it would be wise to inundate them with too much information because they are already overwhelmed."

"That sounds reasonable," continued Dr. Richardson. "Upon completion of the training, they will begin departmental implementation. This will involve the use of these status boards. The intent here is to change the staff's experiences, with the hopes of changing their beliefs and behaviors."

Nick interrupted, "It will also allow both the staff and management to become familiar with Lean tools in a nonthreatening environment."

"Okay, I can understand that. Now, I have some notes here. You talked about let me see," Dr. Richardson started flipping through his notes. "Oh yes, here it is. You said 'our processes are not standardized, they are not user-friendly, and they are plagued with obstructions to flow.' Can you explain this in more detail?"

Nick activated the projector and pulled up the slide displaying the house of Lean. He explained that building a Lean enterprise is analogous to building a house. "The key to a strong house is the foundation. If the foundation is weak, the house will crumble. The foundation for a Lean organization is standard work, user-friendliness, and unobstructed throughput." He then explained each in more detail and clarified the four supporting elements and the system.

Dr. Richardson sat quietly reviewing the slide. He then looked around the room and declared, "I like it! I think it just might work."

Ray sat up in his chair. He quickly looked around the room and saw that the other board members were all nodding in agreement. He knew that trying to dispute the plan at this point would only be counterproductive. When Dr. Richardson asked that all those in favor of the plan raise their hand, Ray did so along with all the other board members, although grudgingly.

Ray had an idea. "Congratulations Nick! I do have one last question, however. Obviously, this is not going to come without a price tag. What will you need to make this work?"

"For starters," Nick began, "Donna has just returned from a conference and believes she has found someone to conduct the training for management. We will be developing and conducting the overview training for the staff ourselves. We're not sure what the cost will be. However, Donna said that he is reasonably priced. We should have some numbers by next week."

"Is that it?"

"No. In addition, we would like to rehire staff to get operations up and running."

"How many people are you thinking?"

"We've calculated that to get operations up and running again, we will need eighteen FTEs."

Immediately, everyone started murmuring. Nick looked over at Ray who was smirking again. "Before we make any decisions, please let me explain the rationale behind this request." The grumbling began to settle down, and Nick continued. "We have demonstrated that over the past three years, errors have been on the increase. We believe this increase is directly linked to layoffs. When we reduce the work force, in an effort to cut costs, the responsibilities associated with these jobs remain. The work still needs to get done, and that obligation often falls to the clinical staff. Consequently, this situation introduces much waste into the process. For example, I observed a patient who had to be transported from a nursing unit to x-ray. Transport was so short-staffed that a nurse ended up transporting the patient. This does not seem to be a big issue on the surface. However, if we look at the sequence of activities that led to this action, you will see that it is extremely wasteful. What actually happened was, the nurse asked the unit clerk to call transport. Some time later, she checked on her patient and found that the patient had not yet left. Again, the nurse went to the nurse's station and requested that the unit clerk call transport. The same progression occurred two more times, until finally, the nurse made the decision to transport the patient herself. However, the story doesn't end there. A short time later, a transport tech arrived on the unit only to be informed that the nurse transported the patient herself and that his services were no longer required. This simple example demonstrates several categories of waste. There is the obvious waste of the nurse transporting the patient. In addition, there is the waste associated with the nurse continually checking to see if transport had taken her patient, the waste associated with the unit clerk having to stop what she was doing to call transport several times, and the waste associated with the transport tech finally making his way up to the unit only to be told that his services were no longer needed. In addition to the waste, this situation resulted in a delay in patient care. It intensifies animosity between departments, which, in turn, reinforces departmental silos. Most importantly, this situation robs the nurse of precious time, possibly leading to an error or depriving another patient of high-quality care.

"Furthermore, when we compare the salaries of operations staff to that of the clinical staff, the clinical staff may be paid two or three times more. We are being penny wise and dollar foolish. To summarize, by not having operations sufficiently staffed, we increase the possibility of errors, fortify departmental silos, and introduce waste into our processes.

"We estimated the cost of hiring eighteen FTEs to be approximately seven hundred and fifty thousand dollars. As we revealed earlier, the cost accompanying hospital-acquired infections last year was almost two million dollars."

"So are you guaranteeing that if we agree to hire these FTEs, we will have zero HAIs?" asked Ray, mischievously.

"You know that I can't make a guarantee like that. However, I will guarantee that we will experience a significant decrease in the number of errors overall."

"Define significant."

"At least fifty percent." As he said this, he glanced over at his team and received reassuring nods from Donna, Megan, and Elizabeth.

"We're not in the gambling business. You're asking us to risk three-quarters of a million dollars on a hunch that errors will decrease, and, if they don't go down, then what? Then, we've lost the bet, and these poor people have to experience the humiliation of another layoff."

Jim Donahue said, "Hold on, Ray! What Nick is saying makes a lot of sense, and he has data to substantiate it. I know that distractions are a leading cause of errors in healthcare, and due to a lack of staffing in operations, it sounds like these nurses are constantly distracted. I remember reading about a hospital that had what they called 'quiet zones.' The inpatient units put tape on the floor around certain areas, and when the nurses were in these areas, no one was permitted to disturb them. I don't remember the exact numbers, but this hospital did have a significant reduction in the number of medication errors.

"The problem is our nurses are not getting distracted by others. They are getting distracted because the processes are not user-friendly!" continued Jim. "Unless we staff operations so that the nurses don't have to perform these superfluous duties, I believe that errors will continue to rise."

"Are you telling me that you're in favor of granting this request to add eighteen FTEs?" asked Ray incredulously.

"Absolutely! Everything that has been presented here this evening makes perfect sense. I agree that we are caught in a cycle that is worsening our financial situation rather than alleviating it. I agree that before anything can change for the better, we must first instill a new culture in which the patient comes first. I agree that the hospital must operate as a system where everyone is working together for the good of the patient. These things cannot happen if we maintain the current staffing levels. We need to grab the bull by the horns and start dealing with the source of the problem rather than the symptoms."

Ray didn't have a response. He simply shook his head and looked down at his notes. Susan agreed with Jim's statement, and Dr. Richardson put it to a vote. The request was approved.

After the meeting, the leadership team adjourned to Nick's office. Ron was ecstatic, "I can't believe it! This will make such a difference for my departments."

"Not just your departments," added Megan. "The nurses and techs will actually be able to focus more on patient care."

"Hold on!" said Elizabeth. "I don't want to take the wind out of everyone's sails, but we need to roll this out properly. If we don't, we may find ourselves in the same situation that got us in this mess."

"You're absolutely right, Elizabeth, but for now let's just enjoy the moment. We can talk about rolling this out on Monday," said Nick.

The team spent some time relishing the outcome of their efforts over the past two weeks. Eventually, they all headed home.

Chapter 14

No Time to Celebrate

Nick had a very relaxing weekend and felt energized on Monday morning when he arrived at his office. "Congratulations!" said Betty. "I was so glad to hear that you got the approval for the plan."

Nick smiled and shook his head. "Betty, how is it that you know what's happening before everyone else?"

"If I told you, it would be the last time I got any firsthand information."

"That's legitimate," said Nick with a shrug.

"I took the liberty of scheduling a rollout meeting for eleven to one today. I ordered lunch from the sandwich shop down the street."

"Betty, you're truly amazing. Thank you," said Nick as he headed for his office.

At eleven o'clock, the entire senior leadership team was sitting around the conference table, smiling from ear to ear. Nick started the meeting by once again thanking everyone for the effort they each made over the past two weeks. He then turned to Elizabeth and asked for her thoughts about rolling out the Lean initiative.

"I don't have anything specific. I just know that we need to do this in an organized way, making sure that the staff understands that it's not going to be business as usual. Things are going to be changing, and they need to be willing to change with them."

"Agreed," said Nick. "I'm thinking we can have a series of *town hall*-type meetings and explain the plan to the staff. I want to be completely transparent. We should explain the situation, introduce the plan, and then deliver the good news."

"I think we should acknowledge the hard work of the entire staff," added Megan. "Everyone, regardless of his or her job description, has been doing whatever is necessary to get the job done. They are all stressed and frustrated, but they continue to do their very best. We should acknowledge this to demonstrate that we know they are not to blame for the financial losses."

Nick jotted down Megan's comment on his note pad and asked, "Then what?"

Elizabeth said, "Then, we acknowledge our mistakes. It has become obvious that the patient is no longer our priority. Our focus on finances has led to some bad decisions. The quality of care has been declining. Our processes are not standardized, nor are they user-friendly. Worst of all, we have failed to recognize that our people are our greatest asset."

Nick was feverishly taking notes, trying to keep up. "This is the perfect segue for introducing our plan. First, I want to make it crystal clear that the patient must be our priority. I will explain that we need to get back to our roots and create a system where everyone is working together for the good of the patient."

"They know that! The patient has always been their first priority!" stated Megan. "Everything they do is linked to doing what is best for the patient."

"You're right! However, what they don't know is that we share that commitment to the patient. They think that we don't care about the patient and are totally absorbed by the finances. Everything we have done up until now has substantiated this belief: purchasing inferior supplies because they cost less, reducing the work force to improve the bottom line, dismissing errors without root cause analysis, and ignoring their suggestions for improvement. We need to let them know that we share their commitment to the patient. We will be purchasing better supplies, hiring people to fill the vacancies created by the layoffs, conducting root cause analysis for all errors, and taking appropriate action to address their concerns."

"This would be a good point to introduce the status boards," said Elizabeth.

"Not yet!" countered Donna. "Before we introduce the status boards, the directors and managers must be trained in Lean. We want them to be able to guide their staff in the implementation of Lean tools."

"How soon can we get this consultant in to conduct the training?" asked Nick.

"I'll call him after the meeting and see when we can get him in here to discuss the training."

"Well, what do we do in the meantime?" asked Nick.

"We roll it out. We need to let people know we're implementing Lean and explain why this time it's going to be different, let them know that they will all receive training, et cetera," replied Elizabeth.

"And start filling those vacancies," added Ron. "It's going to take some time to get people back or hire and train new people. The sooner we can get the ball rolling, the sooner operations will be up and running again."

"We can also get the status board printed up," added Donna. "That's also going to take time. When the training is complete, the boards should be ready to go up."

Nick looked over at Betty and asked her to set up some town hall meetings as soon as possible. "Preferably this week. Thursday, Friday, and Monday would work well. We'll need to start early to include the night shift before they go home and stay a little late to do the evening shift. That gives us until Wednesday to refine the presentation," said Nick. "I'll work on it tonight, and we can go over it tomorrow."

Later in the day, Donna came to Nick's office to let him know that the consultant was available Wednesday afternoon. Nick asked her to have Betty set up a meeting. "Does he understand that this is a preliminary meeting and that we haven't made the decision to go with him?"

"Yes, I made that very clear, but I think he's the right person for the job."

"Good, I'm looking forward to meeting him. Thanks Donna." Nick went back to a pile of work that had accumulated over the past two weeks.

Chapter 15

Meet the New Lean Consultant

Tuesday and Wednesday seemed to drag. There was plenty of work, but Nick wanted to get moving with the plan. He had gone over the kick-off presentation with the team, and they came up with a finished product. He informed his team that he would conduct the presentations, but he wanted everyone with him, at all the presentations, to demonstrate their commitment to the Lean implementation.

Wednesday afternoon, Donna knocked on Nick's open office door. He looked up and saw her standing there with the consultant. "Come on in!" he said. Donna introduced them. They exchanged pleasantries as they sat around the conference table. The rest of the team filed in behind them. "Now that everyone is here, let me introduce Charlie Davis. As you all know, Charlie is the Lean consultant whom Donna met at the conference last week."

Nick turned to Charlie and said, "I know that you and Donna have already discussed our situation, but I'd like to go over it again." Nick talked about the hospital's experience with Janice and explained that he believed the reason for the initiative's failure was improper implementation. He then explained the plan for moving forward. Our focus will be on quality and prioritizing patient care. "I want it to be perfectly clear that we only want you to conduct training. We want the implementation to come from the bottom up." Charlie was smiling and nodding as Nick spoke.

"You're absolutely right!" said Charlie. "Proper implementation is the key to success with Lean. The three components of proper implementation are education in Lean principles, bottom-up implementation, and systems thinking. For some reason, this is very difficult for most leadership teams to accept. They always want to conduct *kaizen* events and forgo these critical steps. Regarding your focus on quality, Lean is all about quality. Most people contribute Toyota's success to the fact that they introduced small, economical cars to the United States during the OPEC oil embargo. Granted, that was a stroke of luck, but it's not the reason for Toyota's success. Initially, consumers purchased Toyota vehicles because they were more economical, but they quickly found that the cars were better built, more reliable, and less prone to breakdown than American-made cars. Toyota's commitment to quality was the real reason for their success, and it still is today. With regard to the training, I conduct a three-day workshop, which includes education in Lean tools, healthcare examples utilizing these tools, and hands-on exercises. Nevertheless, no matter how good the training is, the participants are not going to become Lean experts in three days. I highly recommend, in the beginning, that I be available to provide assistance. I am not talking about implementation, only providing direction with regard to what tool to use and how it works."

"Can you give us an overview of the workshop?" asked Joe.

"Certainly! I begin with terminology. I explain takt time, cycle time, push and pull, and standard work in process and others. I also talk about value-added, business value-added, and non-value-added operations. Next, there are tools in Lean for identifying waste and for eliminating waste. Surprisingly, waste is not always easily identifiable."

"What do you mean?" asked Nick. "I have been observing processes, and I've identified an overabundance of waste."

"I'm sure you have. That's because you have become familiar with the categories of waste and thereby developed an awareness for waste. I would give you odds that before you developed this insight, you could have observed these processes multiple times and never have noticed the waste."

"That's true!" replied Nick. "Still, I don't understand why we need a tool to identify waste. Why can't we just make people aware of the categories of waste?"

"Because we need people to develop a heightened awareness for waste. Waste likes to hide. It disguises itself as work. It's important for people to be aware of this fact. They should understand that being busy and adding value are not synonymous. People can be busy for a good portion of the day and not add any value. They don't identify their actions as waste because it's the way they've always done it. Have you ever heard that explanation?" They all nodded. "When someone says that, it's a clear indication that there is waste in that process. Until we've developed this heightened awareness for waste, we use these tools to help us identify waste in the processes."

"What tools are included in the training?" asked Ron.

"Standard work is the tool we use to identify waste. The other tools are for eliminating waste. They include 5S, *kanbans*, visual controls, mistake proofing, quick changeover, and an introduction to Six Sigma. I conclude the training by explaining how to conduct a *kaizen* event."

"Standard work is a tool?" asked Megan.

"Yes, it's different from the term used to identify standardized process steps. Standard work employs forms to identify wasteful process steps, ascertain the distribution of work, and emphasize the waste of excess motion."

"What about value stream mapping?" asked Donna. "That was the first thing that our other consultant told us we had to do."

"I'm very glad that you asked that question. Value stream maps or VSMs are extremely useful in manufacturing. Unfortunately, that is not the case in healthcare. In healthcare, the process map makes much more sense. The rationale for this belief is that in manufacturing, a specific product is being made, such as a car. They may be different models, have different features, even different colors, but they are all cars. In healthcare, however, a service is being provided rather than a product being built. Unlike cars, every patient is different and requires different services. Even if the service falls into the same category, say, surgery, the VSM is not an appropriate tool because it does not have a logic operator. Let me explain. A logic operator allows me to ask a question. Let's use the surgery example. My first question would be, what type of surgery? Let's assume it is orthopedic surgery. This leads to the next question, what type of orthopedic surgery is being performed? Let's say total joints. Again, this leads to another question, which joint, knee or hip? You would have to have a separate map for each type of surgery. Try to imagine how many different value stream maps there are in healthcare. In addition, the VSM does not take into account things like comorbidities, allergies, or medications. In contrast to the VSM, the process map has a logic operator, which allows for these types of questions. It also includes much more detail. The VSM highlights obstructions to flow. Hence, it may be of some value further down the road, but for right now, I believe the process map is much more valuable.

"Now that you mention it, our other consultant had us spend quite a bit of time drawing these value stream maps, and we never really did anything with them," recalled Donna. "They looked impressive, but I can see how a process map might have been much more useful."

"What about tools that are not specific to Lean? I'm referring to tools that the staff here might be familiar with or possibly might have employed in the past. Cause-and-effect diagrams, failure mode and effect criticality analysis, Pareto diagrams, affinity diagrams, et cetera," asked Megan. "Will you be covering any of those topics during the training?"

"I cover all of those tools in the mistake-proofing portion of the training. I also discuss A3 reports and explain Japanese terminologies such as *jidoka, heijunka, kaizen, andon, gemba,* and others. I try to stay away from the Japanese terms, but it is important for people to know what they mean."

"Especially for us," said Nick as he opened his folder and handed Charlie a copy of their house of Lean.

Charlie looked it over and said, "This is perfect. The ultimate goal in Lean is to create flow, and the three things necessary for flow are standard work, user-friendliness, and unobstructed throughput. These are the three things we want everyone in the organization to internalize. I am also glad that you recognize respect for people as a supporting element. Most organizational leaders don't walk the talk regarding respect for people, which brings me to another important point. I would like to begin by conducting training for the senior leadership team. I want to make sure that you understand your role in the implementation. Also, it is important that you can speak the language. Some consultants will suggest that you come to work in jeans and participate in a 5S activity. I don't agree with that. I think your time is better spent running the organization. However, it's important for you to understand the tools and concepts. The training is only about six hours, but I believe it is important."

"I agree," said Nick. "Just in this short time we've been talking, I've picked up a few things that I was not aware of. What is your availability?"

"I can begin next week, and I am free for the following two weeks. After that, I will be working with another organization for two weeks, but I can come back here when I'm done."

"That sounds perfect. Donna will be in touch with you if we decide to move forward." Nick thanked him for his time and escorted him to the elevator, where they parted company.

Back in his office, the team made the decision to hire Charlie. Nick told Donna to make the arrangements and for each member of the team to make arrangements for their directors and managers to attend.

Chapter 16

Kick-Off Meetings

Thursday morning, the leadership team was present in the auditorium before seven o'clock for the first of twelve kick-off meetings. Attendance was a bit sparse, and Nick asked Donna if the meetings were mandatory. "Yes, but keep in mind that it's seven in the morning. Most of the people here are just coming off the night shift, and the rest haven't started work yet."

"Well that explains why so many of them have their eyes closed."

"Also, remember that they think they're here to hear you announce another layoff."

"Maybe if I begin with that, it will pique their interest." He turned and faced his audience.

"Good morning! You probably think that you are here this morning so I can explain how, once again, the hospital is having financial difficulties and that we need to do some restructuring. Well, I am very happy to tell you that this is not the case. We will not be having another layoff." Some people opened their eyes and became a bit more attentive. "Today, we are here to announce a new direction for the organization. We, in senior leadership, have made some bad decisions in the past that have made your jobs very difficult. Because of these decisions, you have had to assume additional duties, work harder, and deal with a lot of stress and frustration. In spite of these adversities, you have always managed to get the job done, and for that I am sincerely thankful.

"In addition, our emphasis on finances has caused us to neglect our real obligation, which is to provide high-quality patient care. Our patients must and will receive the best possible care that we can provide. To accomplish this, we have developed a plan for moving forward. There are several components to this plan, all of which are directed toward providing high-quality care for our patients. We recognize that our processes are broken. To fix our processes, we need to first comprehend how these processes operate, not a superficial understanding but a meticulously detailed appreciation for how they work. We need to develop the kind of understanding that comes from actually carrying out these duties on a daily basis for months or even years. This is the kind of familiarity that you have with your processes. No one knows these processes better than you. You know the ins and outs, what has gone wrong in the past, and what might go wrong in the future. You know who to go to when you need something done. You also know what the problems are, and you might even have some ideas about how to fix these problems. With your help, and the support and guidance of management, we will begin to fix these processes." More people began to become engaged. Everyone was sitting up, and no one had their eyes closed.

"We will be employing Lean tools and principles to create standard work to make our processes user-friendly and to eliminate bottlenecks." With this announcement, people began to converse, and the murmur began to grow louder. Nick put up his hands and said, "Before you make any judgments, please hear me out! We will be employing Lean tools and principles. We are not contracting a consultant to implement Lean. Instead, you will work closely with your management to apply these principles. Everyone will be receiving training in the Lean methodology. Directors and managers will receive the most comprehensive training, and the staff will receive an overview. We have contracted with a consultant to conduct the training, but he will not be doing any implementation. He has recommended that we make his services available to assist management in the application of these tools. However, we have decided to make this service available only if requested by management.

"Finally, we know that the layoffs have left the organization extremely shorthanded. To alleviate some of the problems that the restructuring has created, we will be restaffing operations. We are currently in the process of bringing people back or hiring new people to fill these vacated positions." Someone in the back row began to clap. Nick shielded his eye from the light and saw that it was Loretta Lewis. She began to clap louder, and others joined in until everyone was applauding. When the applause subsided, Nick asked if there were any questions. The first question had to do with whether or not Janice Brown was returning. Nick assured everyone that she would not be coming back. There were questions about when the implementation of this plan would begin. Nick explained that it was necessary to complete the training before doing any implementation and that the training was scheduled to begin next week. The majority of the inquiries had to do with when the operations people would be starting and who would be coming back. Nick answered these questions as best as he could, and the meeting was adjourned.

The next meeting was scheduled for ten o'clock. Nick and his team arrived at nine forty-five and found the auditorium filled to capacity. People were standing along the sidewalls and were stacked three deep in the back. "I guess they liked what you had to say at the last meeting," Donna said to Nick as they walked toward the stage. "News spreads pretty rapidly around here, whether it's good or bad."

"Well, it's nice to be delivering good news for a change," replied Nick. "Everyone was due for a break from the usual bad news. I know I certainly was. It looks like Megan was right when she said that quality was something people can get fired up about."

Megan was behind them and overheard his comment. "Hey, I'm a nurse, too. People seem to forget that. I know what's important to the staff, and it's definitely not making more money for the organization." She turned to Joe and mouthed "no offense."

Joe smiled and said, "None taken."

Elizabeth said, "I don't know if you realize it, but we have just taken the first step toward changing the organizational culture. The behavior exhibited by the staff at the last meeting was to make an appearance but not necessarily pay attention. This behavior was based on their belief that they were just going to hear more of the same. However, the experience was different from what they expected. Nick, you just changed their experiences, and look at the results. The room is full! When was the last time that happened?"

"Never, not since I've been here!" replied Nick.

They finished the last of the twelve kick-off meetings on Monday evening. Charlie was scheduled to do the leadership overview on Tuesday at nine and then conduct the first workshops on Wednesday, Thursday, and Friday. Things were moving along nicely, but they were still weeks away from putting the plan into action. Nick was chomping at the bit to get things moving, but he knew how important it was to implement Lean in the proper sequence.

Chapter 17

Training

Charlie began the executive overview training at nine o'clock on Tuesday morning, as scheduled. He opened with the definition of Lean. "Lean is a system for the absolute elimination of waste. There are two key words in this definition. The first is system, and I believe that you already recognize the importance of working as a system. The second key word is absolute and refers to the fact that no one is exempt from the task of identifying waste. Your reaction to what I just said has probably conjured up thoughts of the people at the bottom of the organizational pyramid. And you would be correct. These people are not exempt. However, I was referring to the top of the pyramid, as well, the people in this room. You are not exempt from the task of identifying waste. This means the initiative cannot be delegated. Senior leadership likes to delegate. You cannot hire or assign someone to be responsible for Lean. Lean is everyone's responsibility. Also, Lean cannot be consultant driven, which I think you have learned for yourselves from your previous experience with a Lean consultant. Lastly, Lean cannot be purchased. It is serious business and requires hard work. That said, before we go any further, I want to make sure that you understand that Lean is not a quick fix, a silver bullet, or a magic potion. You are embarking on a journey to transform the organization."

"How long will it take to become a Lean organization?" asked Nick.

"Well, you don't actually become a Lean organization. You strive to become a Lean organization; it's continuous improvement. In reality, becoming a Lean organization would lead to complacency. You can never become complacent. The second that you lean back and put your feet up on your desk, you begin to backslide. The tag line for Toyota's luxury vehicle division, Lexus, is 'the pursuit of perfection.' That's the goal. There is no end. Instead, you must continually try to be the best that you can."

"Then, let me rephrase the question. When can we expect to see some benefits associated with the Lean initiative?"

"Almost immediately. From what you've told me, you have already experienced benefits in the nuclear stress test, CT, ED, and on the units. Lean tools and principles will provide an abundance of benefits. However, improving the processes is relatively easy and is not the challenge. The real challenge is sustaining the gains. Almost anyone can apply these tools and principles and articulate the gains resulting from applying them. Regrettably, these are unrealized gains. They are the gains the organization would experience, if the changes were upheld. You've already experienced this tendency in the nuclear stress test. You implemented one-piece flow, and the benefits were immediately apparent. Yet, without the oversight of the director, the gains would have slipped away. Regrettably, try as they might, management cannot enforce these changes. It would require full-time surveillance to ensure the staff is adhering to the standard work.

"Your plan recognizes that training in Lean principles, bottom-up implementation, and systems thinking is the key to success. Training and bottom-up implementation are essential to changing the culture, and systems thinking will eliminate silos. This is why I am so excited to be here, but please understand it is going to require hard work, and it will take time."

"Let's talk about that for a minute," said Nick. "We have conducted a kick-off meeting to let everyone know that we will be implementing Lean. You will be conducting the workshops, and we will provide a Lean overview for the staff. Once the training is complete, we will hang the status boards and begin implementing Lean tools and principles. How long should we keep the boards up?"

"Indefinitely! The status boards are the organization's link between staff and management. They are the catalyst for change. The entire initiative is built around these boards. Why would you want to take them down?"

"Well, I would predict that at some point, people are going to run out of issues to put on the board."

"I can assure you that there will always be issues. In the beginning, you're going to get a lot of ideas. Your people can't wait to tell you what's wrong with your processes because no one has been willing to listen to them until now. The quantity of ideas will decrease over time, and eventually they will stop altogether. The reason they will stop is that in the beginning, the staff will be identifying obvious waste. However, remember what I said about waste? Waste likes to hide! They won't see that hidden waste unless you make them aware of it, and you do this by providing training. They must be taught to see the waste that is not so apparent. Shigeo Shingo said, 'The greatest waste is the waste that we don't see.' Let me give you an example of how we create layers of work for ourselves and never associate it with waste. Imagine a nurse; she can be working anywhere in the hospital on a unit, in the ED, in surgery, it doesn't matter. She needs some supplies to assist a doctor with a procedure and walks to the supply room to get what she needs. When she gets there, the supplies are not on the shelf where they are supposed to be. So, now she must search for the supplies. That's an added layer of work, but it doesn't stop there. She can't find the supplies in the room, so she calls the storeroom to have some delivered, another layer of work. No one answers the phone, but she needs the supplies, so she travels down to the storeroom, another layer of work. When she arrives at the storeroom, she is informed that the item she is looking for is on backorder and won't be available for at least two weeks. She now must go back to the unit and tell the doctor that they don't have the necessary supplies to conduct the procedure. The doctor gets angry. The nurse gets embarrassed and vows that this will never happen again. To prevent this scenario from recurring, she starts conducting regular inventories at the end of each day, another layer of work. She makes a list of all the supplies that need to be replenished and calls the storeroom and orders the supplies, another layer of work. The supplies are delivered in the evening, so the nurse comes in early so she can stock the supplies in their proper location, another layer of work. So you can see how unknowingly we create layers of work for ourselves by incorporating work-arounds and stopgap measures, but let me get back to the example. The nurse continues this process for a few years, and they hire another nurse. How does she train him? She tells him that every night before he leaves, he needs to conduct an inventory of supplies. Then, she instructs him to order any supplies that need to be replenished and come in early the next day to stock the supplies. He does it for a few years, and they hire another nurse. How does he train her? The same way! These layers of work have become standard work. When you ask people why they are conducting this cumbersome process, they say, 'That's the way we've always done it.' As I mentioned earlier, that statement is a clear indicator of a process laden with waste. Now comes the question that will get to the point of this example. How does the staff identify with these wasteful operations? They don't categorize these extra duties as waste. Conversely, they believe that by conducting these additional steps, they are doing a good job. Typically, their boss classifies these actions the same way. Until they receive training, they will never even assume that these process steps might be wasteful, and if you attempt to eliminate these steps, they will resist."

Megan asked, "Are you suggesting that we put everyone through this three-day workshop?"

"No, the staff is already too overwhelmed. What I recommend is monthly training, during regularly scheduled staff meetings. This training should not take more than ten or fifteen minutes. It is very important that it be scripted. The reason being, if you were to ask ten different directors to explain a *kanban*, you would probably get ten different interpretations. By scripting the training, everyone is getting the same information, not someone's interpretation of the topic." Charlie walked over to the flip chart and grabbed a marker. "Let's say this month's training is related to the waste of excess motion. We must first define what we mean by excess motion. It is defined as any unnecessary staff movement. We then clarify the definition. Unnecessary staff movement involves unwarranted walking, searching, or small movements such as logging onto computers. Next, we give some examples of excess motion like searching for patient charts or having to log onto multiple computer systems to obtain information. Then, we discuss the tool for identifying excess motion, which is the standard work form, and we explain how to use the form. Next, we discuss a tool for eliminating the waste of excess motion. There are several tools that can be used to eliminate excess motion, so we introduce one each month. For the first session, let's use physical layout. I'm not going to go into detail, but physical layout is basically having the workplace laid out in a way that is most conducive to work. Then, the person conducting the training can go around the room and ask each participant to provide an example of excess motion in their area. If there are ten people in the room, and each person gives one example, there are ten opportunities to eliminate waste. I would then tell each person to put the waste on the status board." Charlie had scripted their first training session.

EXCESS MOTION

DEFINITION: Unnecessary staff movement
        Walking
        Searching
        Logging onto computer

EXAMPLE: Searching for patient charts

TOOL FOR ID: Standard Work Form

TOOL TO ELIMINATE: Physical Layout

**HAVE PARTICIPANTS GIVE EXAMPLES OF
EXCESS MOTION IN THEIR AREA**

Charlie went on to discuss some Lean terminology. He began with takt time, which is the rate of customer demand. "Takt time tells me how much time I have to process each patient or product. Cycle time tells me how long it takes to process one patient or product. So my rule is that my takt time must be less than my cycle time. Calculating takt time should be one of the first things we do. Everything we do to improve a process should be based on takt time. We calculate our takt time by dividing the available time by customer demand. Then, we obtain cycle time through observation. If my cycle time is greater than my takt time, I cannot meet my customer demand and must take appropriate action to modify my process. We should first look for opportunities to eliminate wasteful process steps. If that doesn't alleviate the problem, we might need to add overtime or increase staffing. Perhaps we can combine the process with another process that has a cycle time that is less than the takt time."

He went on to explain one-piece flow and standard work in process or SWIP. "SWIP is the minimum number of parts or patients necessary to ensure flow."

"Wait a minute!" said Ron. "You're saying that we should insert inventory into our processes to allow them to flow? Isn't inventory considered waste?"

"Yes, it is. However, if your process is not balanced, meaning that some operations take longer than others, it may be necessary to add inventory to create flow. SWIP is the minimum amount of inventory we can have and still allow the process to flow. However, before we add SWIP, we should try to balance the process. We can do this by eliminating wasteful process steps, redefining process steps, combining operations, adjusting staffing, or whatever else we can think of."

"Let me see if I understand this," said Nick. "If I have a process consisting of three operations, and operation one takes five minutes, operation two takes ten minutes, and operation three takes five minutes, should I combine operations one and three?"

"That's one possibility. However, remember that everything we do is based on our takt time. If your takt time is five minutes, you won't be able to meet your customer demand because your cycle time is ten minutes. So there are two things you can do. Do you see what they are?"

"Yes, I can split the ten-minute operation and have two five-minute operations, or I can add a second process."

"Correct! Now keep in mind that in real-life situations, things are not going to be as simple and straightforward as these examples. But don't give up because almost any process can flow. It just takes time and persistence."

Charlie explained the different standard work forms and what they were used for. He then went on to explain the other tools associated with Lean. When he was done, Nick said, "This is a lot of information! I think that if management doesn't start applying these tools right away, they will forget the majority of it. But the status boards won't be up for at least a few months. What can management do in the meantime to retain what they've learned?"

"Excellent question! I would suggest that each director or manager create a detailed process map of all the processes for which they have responsibility. The workshop includes a section on process mapping. This section is not about creating a basic process map. Instead, I demonstrate how to create a very useful process map that utilizes three different mapping strategies. The finished product not only shows the flow of the process. It also highlights problem areas; identifies bottlenecks; and classifies process steps as value added, business value added, or non-value added. In addition, it provides information relative to each operation such as cycle time, takt time, staffing requirements, et cetera. They can then address each problem area or bottleneck one at a time. A big problem in both manufacturing and healthcare is that we try to fix the entire process in one shot, and we end up fixing nothing. These problems typically do not have to be addressed in any particular order. So management can pick and choose which ones to work on based on their current workload. They can use individual Lean tools, or they can use them in combination."

When Charlie finished his presentation, he turned off the projector and said, "There is one more thing I would like to cover before we conclude. Leadership's role in ensuring the success of these status boards is critical. You all have busy schedules, and urgent and important matters will take priority over rounding to the boards. This cannot happen! Fortunately, it is not necessary to spend hours rounding to all these boards in a single day. I would recommend that you split up into teams of two and spend fifteen or twenty minutes at the beginning of each day and visit just one board a day. There are six of you. That will allow you to visit three boards a day, fifteen a week, or sixty a month. I cannot overemphasize the importance of this segment of the plan. The people in this room are the only people in the organization with the authority to address barriers to change. If you are negligent in conducting daily rounding, the initiative will fail."

Over the next couple of months, Charlie conducted the Lean workshops. Many managers requested his assistance in creating their process maps, calculating takt times, and obtaining cycle times. They all benefited greatly from his assistance, and in a couple of hours, they were able to proceed on their own. Senior leadership began spending their spare time, as scarce as it was, in the departments providing whatever support they could. They saw detailed process maps and standard work forms hanging on office and break-room walls. Many departments had conducted 5S events. These departments were uncluttered, neat, clean, and organized. The staff members were excited about the improvements. They were making comments such as, 'I can easily find the supplies I need,' 'I'm not wasting my time looking for equipment,' and 'I'm not tripping over stuff that we don't need.' In the training, Charlie had said that 5S was a great tool for introducing Lean concepts. The benefits were immediately obvious. The standard work was straightforward and easy to follow, "If you use it, put it away. If you spill it, clean it up. If you break it, get it fixed." Most importantly, the fifth S, sustain the gains, helped build the discipline needed to become a Lean organization.

With the return of the operations staff, risk management had already reported a decrease in the number and severity of errors. Quality indicators were improving, and patient satisfaction was on the rise. "We haven't even conducted the staff overview yet, and the benefits are already apparent," said Nick, as he and Donna walked together while visiting one of the units.

"I know! I spoke with Sara Sullivan today. She's the director of Laboratory Services. She has been requesting that I hire a phlebotomist for the outpatient blood draw area. I told her that aside from restaffing operations, we decided not to hire people as a solution to our problems. The area has two registrars, one phlebotomist, and a volunteer who works as a receptionist. After going through the Lean workshop, she completed her process map and reviewed it with the staff to determine if they could find an alternate solution. One of the registrars suggested that she be cross-trained, which is something they often do in Lean, as a phlebotomist. In turn, she would train the phlebotomist to register patients. They set up the blood draw areas with computer terminals from the registrar's offices, and now the patients are registered, and their blood is drawn all in one location."

"Are they able to meet demand now?" asked Nick.

"Not only are they meeting the demand for blood draws, but also they freed up the other registrar to work upstairs in the laboratory. So, not only did they not hire someone to solve their problem, but they also picked up an additional FTE in the department."

"I must say, I am very impressed with everything that is going on. We're seeing a lot of improvements, and morale is improving," Nick stated.

"Morale isn't just improving. People are excited! I will walk into an area, and staff members will come up to me and tell me how much better the working conditions are."

"Monday we begin the staff overviews and we'll be hanging the status boards. I hope we get the same response from the staff as we got from management!"

Chapter 18

Staff Overview

Monday morning saw the first of the staff overviews. The session was full, especially considering the early hour. The leadership team decided to conduct the hour-long overview in ten-minute segments so they could all participate. Nick began with a greeting and by once again thanking everyone for their dedication to their patients. He then provided the definition of Lean that Charlie had provided, spoke about the two key words, and explained about layers and how waste likes to hide.

Megan was next. "I'm going to talk about the waste in our processes. When Donna first introduced the idea of Lean and eliminating waste, I was offended. I immediately went on the defensive, insisting that our processes were waste free. To my surprise, I was proven wrong. Our processes are complex, outdated, and laden with unnecessary, wasteful steps." To help everyone better understand waste, she had prepared an exercise. Working with the director of the Emergency Department, Megan recorded the process for admitting a patient with community-acquired pneumonia, from the time the patient presented in the ED to the time they left the ED to go to the unit. The process consisted of thirty steps. She had the participants read the steps and put the step in one of three categories. The first category was *value added*. She defined this category as tasks that are contributing to making the patient well. The next category was *business value added* or things that do not contribute to making the patient well but are necessary for care to be delivered. The last category was *non-value added*. "These are tasks that do not add value from the standpoint of either the patient or the business, and they're neither necessary nor required." She allowed everyone some time to complete the task and then asked for a show of hands as to how many people identified half, fifteen, or more of the steps as value added. No one raised their hand. She then asked for twelve, ten, and eight. Still, no one raised their hand. At five, most people raised their hand. She then pulled up a PowerPoint slide, listing the five steps that she had categorized as adding value. She explained that these five steps, on average, took one hour. The entire process was eleven hours, yet, only one hour could be contributed to making the patient well. "Although some of these tasks can be categorized as business value added, the majority fall into the category of non-value added. These third-category tasks are what we are referring to when we say waste."

She then went on to talk about the implications of the exercise. "Everyone is working very hard, they are dealing with very real problems, and they are trying to solve these problems as quickly as they can. As a result, they are stressed and frustrated, but they are not adding value. What they are doing is trying to force a complex and outdated care delivery system to run smoothly." She paused for effect and added, "It's not going to happen! Trying harder is not going to get us where we need to be. Everyone is trying harder. They're taking on additional tasks and doing whatever is necessary to deliver the prescribed care to their patients." Again, she paused and then said, "But trying harder is not going to get us there! We must eliminate the waste from our processes." She then explained that many of the work-arounds and stopgap measures that they have added to their processes have caused waste to be an accepted or even required component.

Joe was next. He surprised everyone when he told the participants that their focus going forward must be on quality and not finance. He explained how focusing on finances has led to bad decisions. He displayed his *Reactive Cycle for Dealing with Financial Instability* and explained how their bad decisions had led to poor quality, which in turn caused financial instability. He presented the hospital-acquired infection statistics and Megan's graph demonstrating the correlation between layoffs and errors. He went on to explain the seven wastes, giving definitions and examples of each. He also told them that they would be receiving short training modules during their monthly staff meetings.

Elizabeth explained the need for systems thinking. She defined silos and all the issues associated with silos. She also spoke about the importance of developing a Lean culture. "We must develop a culture where everyone is on the lookout for anything that might jeopardize patient quality or patient safety. In addition, we must all acquire a heightened awareness for waste." She explained that building a Lean organization is analogous to building a house. "When we build a house, we must have a blueprint. We want to know the size of the house, the layout, the orientation, et cetera. For a Lean organization, the blueprint is our strategic plan. We will be assigning strategically focused, patient-centered objectives to department management, obliging them to work as a system. Management will be held accountable for these objectives, meaning that their performance will be evaluated on how well they worked together for the good of the patient, not how well their department is doing, thereby eliminating silos." She also introduced the three foundational elements of standard work, user-friendliness, and unobstructed throughput.

Donna was excited about her segment. She was getting to introduce the status boards. She first reviewed what Nick had said at the kick-off meeting. "You are the experts at your jobs.

You know them better than anyone else, and you know what the problems are. We need you to tell us what those problems are, and if you have ideas relating to fixing the problems, we want to know those ideas. The instrument we will be using, for you to alert management to these issues, is called a status board."

A slide appeared on the screen behind her displaying a finished status board. She explained how the board worked and that each person could see that his or her issue is not being ignored. They can see the issue progress through the four phases of the plan, do, study, act cycle. She explained how each person would work together with the support and guidance of management to address the issue and prevent its recurrence. Finally, she explained the three rules, being sure to provide additional clarification to the low-cost rule. "When you leave here and return to your departments, we want you to utilize these boards. If you identify any of the seven wastes, write it on the board. If you witness that staff members are employing different methods to provide a service, write it on the board. That means the process is not standardized. If you go to the supply room, and what you need is not there, write it on the board. That process is not user-friendly. If you are experiencing unnecessary delays, write it on the board. Those delays are obstructing throughput."

When Donna was finished, Nick took over again. "When we were developing this plan, we often talked about those things that were critical to the success of this plan. Quality focus, training, bottom-up implementation, culture change, systems thinking, and developing a heightened awareness for waste all ranked high on our list of priorities. These things are all extremely important to the success of this initiative. However, the thing that is most critical to our success is you. The people sitting in this room will determine the success or failure of our plan. It is the people in this room who held the organization together through our most difficult times, and you are the same people who will make this organization great again. Thank you all, and let's work together to make this happen."

The participants stood and applauded. The excitement in the room was clearly evident. Nick smiled and turned to his senior team seated behind him to share the accolades. When he did, he saw that they were also standing and applauding.

At the end of the day, they had conducted four sessions. They adjourned to Nick's office for a quick review before calling it a day. "I think that went very well," said Donna.

"Very well? It was fantastic!" said Joe.

Nick said, "You know what's really interesting? This entire plan is just common sense. I think it was Frank Lloyd Wright who said, 'There is nothing more uncommon than common sense.' We just proved him correct."

"Let's put a positive spin on that," said Elizabeth. "I prefer a quote from Thomas Edison that I believe is more appropriate. 'The three great essentials to achieve anything worthwhile are hard work, stick-to-itiveness, and common sense.'"

Nick asked if anyone had anything that they wanted to discuss before they called it a night. Megan said, "I spoke with some of my directors, and they all had the same comment. They said people are coming back to the departments after the overview, and they're looking for the status boards. Ron, do you have any idea when they'll be up?"

"My guys in maintenance have been hanging them on all three shifts. They said the most difficult part is finding out where management wants them hung. They already had to go back and move a few. If everyone could tell their supervisor to identify where they want the boards hung and put in a work requisition, it would be very helpful."

"Okay, anything else?" No one had anything to add, and Nick ended the meeting.

Chapter 19

Rounding

A week after the last overview sessions, Nick called his team together for a brief meeting. "Well, it's time to begin rounding. I agree that we should break up into teams of two, as Charlie suggested, and round every day. However, until we get the hang of it, let's round as a group. I'd like to meet in the lobby tomorrow morning at seven-thirty and round to a few departments."

The next morning, they met as scheduled in the hospital lobby and proceeded to Pharmacy only because it was the closest department. When they entered, they did not see a status board and had to ask a pharmacy tech where it was located. The tech pointed toward the offices. They walked over and realized why the board wasn't so noticeable. It was covered with sticky notes highlighting issues. As they read some of the issues and ideas, they were very impressed. Mikka Lee, the Pharmacy director, came over looking quite excited. After greeting the team, she asked that they join her in the break room. On the way there, she signaled to a few others to join them. When everyone was present, Mikka introduced the three Pharmacy techs she had asked to join them: "This is Sara, Carol, and Bill. I am going to let them tell you about an improvement that they initiated. However, first I'd like to give you some background. During the training with Charlie, he was explaining one-piece flow versus batch and queue. He singled out the Pharmacy, saying, 'I can guarantee that we could go down to the Pharmacy any morning and ask what they're doing, and the response will be 'the morning batch!' That got me thinking about reconfiguring the batch preparation schedule." Mikka explained how she discussed the batch process versus one-piece flow with Sara, Carol, and Bill. "They utilized standard work forms to observe the IV admixture process, and they identified several areas of waste. Utilizing Lean tools and the one-piece-flow concept, they incorporated some changes, but I will let them tell you."

Sara began, "We reallocated one of the Pharmacy techs from the night shift to the day shift. This allowed us to enable an order verification system, which we developed. This system completely eliminated the compounding of duplicate or discontinued orders. The quantity of these orders was estimated to be forty-five percent of all the IV admixtures. This change significantly reduced the Pharmacy's workload." She looked at Carol and nodded.

Carol added, "A big problem that exists in the Pharmacy is that if a nurse goes to the pyxis to get a medication, and it is not there, they think they forgot to order it. So they submit another order. We call that a reorder. So in the Pharmacy, we are compounding the reorder when the original order was already prepared and delivered to the unit via the pneumatic tube system. We attempted to get the nurses to check the tube system before placing an order, but they are too busy. We also found that because we are so inundated with medication requests, nurses attempt to expedite their request by entering them into the system as a stat order. I have had days when I log on to my computer, and every order request was red, indicating that it is a stat order. This order verification process significantly reduced the number of false stat requests, enhancing the quality of patient care and improving patient safety."

"How is reducing false stat requests improving patient care?" asked Ron.

"When all the order requests are stat, I cannot differentiate between a true stat order and a false stat order. When this happens, I treat all orders the same. That means that a patient who truly needs their medication stat may not receive it."

Bill continued the narrative. "We estimate that we receive just over five hundred RN-generated IV admixture requisitions daily. That equates to two hundred and twenty-six requisitions that are either duplicates or discontinued medications. The average cost of a requisition is five dollars and seventy-seven cents, which doesn't sound like a lot of money. Not until you multiply it by the number of IV admixtures we are compounding unnecessarily. We calculated the weekly cost for scrapped IV admixtures to be nine thousand and one hundred and twenty-eight dollars. The estimated annual savings is four hundred and seventy-four thousand six hundred and sixty-two dollars!"

Mikka said, "Granted, this is an estimated cost savings, but I believe it to be pretty accurate based on what we've been experiencing. Before this change, at the end of the day, we would have two or three utility carts full of IV admixtures that needed to be scrapped. Now we only have a handful."

Joe asked, "What is the cost to implement these changes?"

"Zero," responded Mikka.

"No additional FTEs? No equipment purchases?" asked Joe incredulously.

"None, we simply reallocated our manpower more appropriately. I must say that I brought up the idea of reconfiguring the batch process, but the credit for the changes belongs to these three people. I showed them how to use the standard work forms to identify the process waste, and they flew with it."

Nick looked at the three of them and said, "Excellent job! I really appreciate your efforts. Thank you very much." As the three of them filed out of the room, each member of the leadership team shook hands and reiterated Nick's sentiments. "I think we should recognize their efforts in some way," said Nick when they were gone. "Maybe we can fund a pizza lunch or something."

"They don't want pizza," said Mikka. "They want a little recognition for their efforts, which they just received. Everyone wants to feel important. They want to feel that they have something of value to contribute. I don't think you want to start rewarding behaviors, or nothing will get done unless there is a reward attached."

"Excellent point!" said Joe.

Nick had an idea. "What if we write thank-you notes? Megan, Pharmacy is your area of responsibility. Maybe you could write a short note thanking them for their effort and ending with something like, 'Keep up the good work!.'"

"I like that idea!" said Mikka. "I'll bet that if you did that and sent it to their home, you would find it hanging on their refrigerator door next to their kids' drawings."

The team left the Pharmacy and decided to go upstairs to an inpatient unit. They were surprised to find the board empty. "Maybe the board just got hung up this morning," said Ron as he called down to maintenance. When he got off the phone, he looked at Nick and said, "The board went up last week."

"That's interesting!" said Nick. "We hadn't considered this scenario."

One of the nurses was walking by, and Megan stopped her. "Hi Ann. Do you have a minute?" The nurse looked very nervous and indicated that she was in the middle of something that couldn't wait. "I guess we make a pretty intimidating group. Why don't the rest of you go on to the next department, and I'll stay behind and see what I can find out. Where are you heading?"

"We'll meet you down in finance," said Joe. "I want to see if my people came up with anything."

Megan went to Brian Johnson's office. Brian was the director of the unit. She knocked on the door, but there was no response. She then tried to open the door, but it was locked. She went into the supply room and found Ann and another nurse in the room having a conversation. They both stopped talking when she entered. Megan asked if they had attended the Lean overview, and they both indicated that they had. "We found it interesting this morning that your status board is empty. Is there a problem?"

The two nurses looked at each other nervously. Ann directed her friend to watch the door and then said, "Megan, we have lots of ideas, and you didn't hear this from me, but we have been told not to put anything on the board."

"By who?" asked Megan.

"Brian. After the training, he said that he didn't want anyone putting issues on the board. It's really frustrating because we have plenty of ideas on how to improve, but we're being stifled. We were so excited after the Lean overview that we couldn't wait to get back to the unit and start posting ideas. When we got here, Brian told us not to put anything on the board."

"Interesting," said Megan. "Thank you for telling me, and rest assured no one will ever know I heard this from you."

Megan caught up with the team in Finance. They were in the middle of a conversation with Pat Dunn, the director of Finance. She was explaining how the insurance company had challenged charges for implants due to lack of documentation. "They challenged twelve separate accounts, all related to implants, and requested a refund of over one hundred and fifty thousand dollars."

"What documentation was missing?" inquired Joe.

"The insurance company reimbursement is based on cost plus other expenses, so an invoice is required. John Enders submitted the issue, and he had already looked into the cause. He found that Surgery and Cardiology provided invoices, which were used to calculate implant costs. However, not all invoices were making it into the patient's medical record. This sparked the refund request, and the insurance company promised that there were more on the way. In addition, he found that the vendor stocks implants in the department for easy access. The vendor invoices only when the implant is used. These invoices were not always reaching Financial Services. John established and implemented a new process to ensure all reimbursable costs are available to billing. His improvement idea not only negated the refund, but it also prevents this issue from recurring. But that's not all! John also found that nine of the twelve accounts were actually underpaid because we never received the vendor invoices for the stocked implants. We were able to rebill the insurance company for more than seventy-five thousand dollars."

"Looks like you need to write a thank you note, Joe," said Megan when they were finished.

"I hope I have to write a lot more. This is great."

They decided that they had done enough rounding for the day. Megan told them that she needed to meet with everyone in Nick's office for a brief meeting. She told them how Brian had told his staff not to put anything on the status board. "I'm not really sure how to handle this. Any ideas?"

Ron said, "If he worked for me, he would be looking for another job!"

"I'm not going to fire him, Ron!" replied Megan. "Brian is one of my best people."

"Is he?" asked Donna. "Jack Welch said that there are four types of people in an organization. There are those who make the numbers and share your vision. These people are the keepers. There are people who don't make the numbers and don't share your vision. That's a no brainer! They have to go. Next, there are people who don't make the numbers, but they share your vision. We want to take the time to develop these people. Lastly, and the most difficult of the four, are the people who consistently make the numbers, but they don't share your vision. He said, 'These people need to go.' It sounds to me like Brian falls into that last category."

"Okay, hold on!" exclaimed Nick. "We're not General Electric. I don't think we need to go around firing people who don't share our vision. Did you talk to Brian about this?"

"No, he wasn't in his office, and as I said, I wasn't really sure how to handle it. I don't want him to know that one of his nurses told me what he said."

"I think the best thing to do is talk to him. Don't let on that anyone said anything. Just ask him why he thinks there aren't any issues posted on the board. See what he says, and go from there."

That afternoon, Megan saw Brian in the cafeteria. She waved him over to her table so they could talk. "How are you, Brian? Is everything okay?"

"Yes, why are you asking?"

"Well, we were rounding to check out the status boards this morning, and we noticed that there weren't any issues posted on your board. Do you have any idea why?"

"Yeah! I told my people not to put anything on the board."

Megan was taken completely by surprise. "Why did you do that?"

"To be perfectly honest, I don't think Lean is applicable on the unit. I think it's great for processes that mimic manufacturing like the Lab or Pharmacy, but I don't think it will work on the unit. I don't want to waste my time, or my staff's time, trying to implement a methodology that won't work."

"What makes you so sure that it won't work?"

"During the training, every time Charlie introduced a new topic, I could come up with all these different scenarios, all the reasons why Lean wouldn't work."

Megan became very serious. "Okay, Brian. I want you to put the same effort that you expended identifying reasons why Lean wouldn't work and come up with reasons why it will work. We need to make this work! I want you to tell your people to get their issues up on the board. If you are having difficulty, we can bring in Charlie to help you, but I want to see issues on the board the next time we come through. This is not a request Brian. You either get on board, or I will find someone who will."

Brian was caught completely off guard. He knew he was one of Megan's best people, and he was always able to challenge requirements, but this was different. He quickly decided to fall in line. "Well, I think it would be helpful if you could bring Charlie in to help. To be honest, I decided early on that Lean was not going to work, and I didn't really pay close attention in the training."

Megan rolled her eyes. "Brian, this is serious business. I want you on my team, and I know if you change your attitude, you will come up with some great stuff. In the meantime, I will make arrangements for Charlie to come in and help you out."

Chapter 20

A Year Later

With a quorum of members present, Chairman Richardson called the board meeting to order. Per the standard agenda, Kathy read the minutes from the previous meeting, which were approved, seconded, and carried unanimously. The meeting proceeded with the administration reports.

Megan was the first up and gave a quality update. The quality/performance improvement dashboard revealed that all the requirements are either being met or surpassed. Patient satisfaction scores are higher than they have been in over four years, and the core measures are good or better in all areas. Medical and medication errors were both significantly lower than the previous year. Falls were still an issue, and Megan talked about some of the steps they were taking to reduce the number of falls.

She wanted to revisit the data she presented when they came to the board for the approval of the plan. "Hospital-associated infections have dropped significantly. We had zero central line-associated bloodstream infections, seven catheter-associated urinary tract infections, two surgical site infections, and only one ventilator-associated pneumonia."

Joe provided the financial report. To everyone's surprise, he didn't bore them with lengthy reports for significant statistics, operating revenues, labor expenses, and nonlabor expenses. He quickly got to the information that everyone wanted to hear. "I am happy to report that the hospital ended the year in the black. Granted, we are not quite where we would like to be, but our net income for the year is seven hundred and thirty-six thousand, four hundred and eighty-two dollars."

Ray asked, "We all know that financial terms can often be misleading. Is this the actual net income, or is it earnings before interest, taxes, depreciation, and amortization?"

"I agree that financial terms can be very misleading, but I am not attempting to misinform. This number is the bottom line," responded Joe as he passed out a packet containing the income statement, the balance sheet, and the statement of cash flow.

It was time for the CEO's report. Nick stood and said, "This has been an exciting year, and we have seen some incredible developments. I am not going to talk about these developments. Instead, I would like the people who are responsible for making them happen tell you themselves."

Nick nodded to Megan who walked over and opened the boardroom doors. In walked eighteen staff members who had been chosen to present issues they had addressed utilizing Lean concepts. The presentations included Sara, Carol, and Bill's reallocation of resources in the Pharmacy. In addition, there were presentations from the Emergency Department, Diagnostic Imaging, Laboratory Services, and Behavioral Health. Ann, the nurse from Brian Johnson's department, spoke about a project, which she suggested, to enhance Nursing Services' ability to be closer to patient rooms and increase the amount of time at the patient's bedside.

After each presentation, the board members applauded and congratulated each of the presenters on their efforts.

After the last presentation, Nick stood. "We are all very excited about this plan. This is only the first year of the Lean initiative, and the improvements have been spectacular. We have some remarkable people working here, as you have just witnessed through their presentations. We are looking forward to the coming year. I've come to realize what really makes an organization successful. Successful organizations recognize that their people are truly their greatest asset. They respect the employee's knowledge of the processes. Management acknowledges that they cannot solve problems on their own because they are not close enough to the problem to know the facts. Successful healthcare organizations know the value of systems thinking. In most organizations, a department is a group of individual contributors who act independently of other groups. Conversely, in healthcare, there needs to be connectivity in what is being done. In order to get the different components of a system to operate efficiently and effectively, there must be a shared objective. In healthcare, that objective is providing the best possible care for our patients. Finally, successful organizations focus on quality. Whether they're in the business of building cars or providing care for patients, poor quality can never be tolerated."

Dr. Richardson said, "This is very impressive, Nick. You've done a remarkable job. You should be proud of yourself."

"Thank you, Dr. Richardson, but I can't take the credit for these successes. Don't misinterpret this as modesty. I would very much like to take the credit, but this was a collaborative effort. Not just between the leadership team and myself but also with every employee in the hospital. This experience has caused me to develop a completely different understanding of what it means to be a leader. To truly be an effective leader, you must first understand that you don't have all the answers and that only by demonstrating respect for people will you be successful."

Dr. Richardson acknowledged Nick's statement and adjourned the meeting. All the board members, including

Ray Driscoll, went up to Nick after the meeting and congratulated him.

Nick left the boardroom and walked into his office. He turned off the motion detector-activated lights. He sat at his desk, in the dark, looking out the window, and savored the moment.

THE ~~END~~

BEGINNING

Index

A

Accountability, 73, 161
Assembly line, 38

B

Batch and queue, 38
Behaviors, 73–74, 76–78, 125
Beliefs, 73–74, 77–78, 125
Berra, Lawrence Peter (Yogi), 39
Blame culture, 69–70, 124, 127;
    see also Culture change
Board meetings, 1–10, 173–176
Bottom-up implementation, 88, 92,
    100, 102, 127, 140, 150
Business value added activities, 160

C

Carbapenem-resistant
    enterobacteriaceae (CRE), 33
Catheter-associated urinary tract
    infections (CAUTI), 32, 68,
    173
C-Diff (*Clostridium difficile*), 33
Central line-associated blood
    stream infection (CLABSI),
    33, 68, 122, 173

Charts, 14
CLABSI (Central line-associated
    blood stream infection), 33,
    68, 122, 173
Clostridium difficile (C-Diff), 33
Continuous improvement, 53, 54,
    91, 150
Cost of external failures, 71
Cost of internal failures, 71
Cost of poor quality, 33, 68
Costs, 32–34, 69–71, 122, 167,
    169–170
Costs of quality, 71
CRE (Carbapenem-resistant
    enterobacteriaceae), 33
Culture change, 61–74, 91, 102,
    123–124, 150; *see also*
    Blame culture
Customer demand, 154
Cycle time, 154

D

Data, 13–14
Defects, 39; *see also Jidoka*
Departmental focus, 54, 83
Diagram, 123

E

Edison, Thomas, 163
Employees
  blame on, 69–70, 124, 127
  experiences, 76–78
  empowerment, 88, 92, 100, 102,
      127, 140, 150
  layoffs, *see* Layoffs
  Lean house, 90
  resistance, 30–31, 74, 105–107,
      170–172
  Respect for People, 95–96, 105
  rewards, 168, 170
  significance, 11–17
  training, *see* Training
  types, 170
Empowerment, *see* Bottom-up
      implementation
Errors, 33–34, 46, 68–69, 122–123
Excessive motion, 39, 41, 42, 153
Experiences, employee's, 76–78
External operations, 117

F

5S, 90, 93, 157
Financial instability, 67–68
Financial stability, 4, 21, 76–78,
      106, 125
Finger pointing, *see* Blame culture
Flow, 36, 103, 143; *see also*
      One-piece flow
Ford, Henry, 38
Ford Motor Company, 38

G

Gemba, 16–17, 49–52
General Motors (GM), 101
Graphs, 14

H

HAI (Hospital-associated
      infections), 33, 68, 122, 173
Heijunka, 90, 103, 105
Hospital indicators, 4
Hospital-associated infections
      (HAI), 33, 68, 122, 173
Hospitals, vii, 22, 54, 66–67, 104

I

Implementation methods, 88
Information dissemination,
      135–137
Inspection cost, 71
Internal operations, 116–117
Inventory, 39, 58, 152, 155; *see also*
      Kanban

J

Jidoka, 90, 94, 105

K

Kaizen, 29, 90, 95, 105, 141–143
Kanban, 90, 113, 119
Kick-off meetings, 145–148

L

Layoffs
  costs and, 68–69
  errors and, 46, 68–69, 122–123
  resistance and, 170–172
  workloads and, 13, 14–15, 46
Layout, physical, 153
Leadership, role, 156; *see also*
      Senior leadership
Leadership commitment, 90

Lean
    challenge, 150
    continuous improvement and,
        150
    definition, 35, 149
    elements, 53, 91; *see also*
        Standard work;
        Unobstructed throughput;
        User-friendliness
    goal, 36, 143
    proper implementation and, 140
Lean consultant, 29–31, 86, 139–144
Lean enterprise, 104, 105
Lean house, 89–96
Lean manufacturing organization,
    90
Lean principles, education in, 140
Logic operators, 142

M

Maltz, Maxwell, 107
Meetings
    board, 1–10, 173–176
    kick-off, 145–148
    overview, 159–163
    senior leadership, 27–37, 44–47,
        52–57, 64–74, 76–88,
        98–105
Methicillin-resistant *Staphylococcus*
    aureus (MRSA), 33
Money, *see* Finance stability
Motion, 39, 41, 42, 153
Muda, see Waste

N

New United Motor Manufacturing
    Incorporated (NUMMI), 101
Non-value added activities, 160;
    see also Waste

O

Observation, 39, 154
Ohno, Taiichi, 39
One-piece flow, 38, 59–60, 63, 166
Operations, 116–118
Organizational culture, 54, 55–56,
    73, 91
Overprocessing, 39, 41
Overproduction, 39, 58
Overview meetings, 159–163

P

Passive resistance, 30–31, 74,
    105–107, 170–172
Patient care, 76–78, 165–167;
    see also Waste
Patient satisfaction, 4, 65
Patients, 67, 124
PD (Positive deviance), 99
PDSA (Plan, do, study, act) cycle,
    81–83
People, *see* Employees
Physical layout, 58
Plan, do, study, act (PDSA) cycle,
    81–83
Poka-yoke, 90
Positive deviance (PD), 99
Postsurgical wound infections, 34
Prevention cost, 71
Process efficiency, 61, 64
Process map, 142, 155–156
Proper implementation, 140

Q

Quality, 4, 66–67, 101–102; *see also*
    Cost of poor quality; Cost
    of quality; *Jidoka*
Quality costs, 71

R

Resistance, passive, 30–31, 74,
    105–107, 170–172
Respect for people, 95–96, 105
Rewards, 168, 170
Rounds, 165–172

S

Save the Children, 98
Scrub phase, 93
Searching, 36
Senior leadership
    meetings, 27–37, 44–47, 52–57,
        64–74, 76–88, 98–105
    roles, 54–55, 80, 83, 91, 128
Services, 142
Shingo, Shigeo, 116, 151
Silos, 54, 83, 91, 124, 127, 150
Single-Minute Exchange of Die
    (SMED), 90, 116–118
Sort phase, 93
SSI (Surgical site infections), 33, 68,
    122, 173
Standard work
    continuous improvement and,
        91
    definition, 53, 141
    5S, 93
    Lean house, 90, 91, 105
    significance, 91, 141
    unobstructed output and, 54
    user-friendliness and, 54, 92
Standard work form, 153
Standard work in process (SWIP),
    90, 154–155
Standardize phase, 93
Staphylococcus aureus infections,
    33, 34
Status boards, 81–85, 127
Sternin, Jerry, 98–100
Straighten phase, 93

Surgical site infections (SSI), 33, 68,
    122, 173
Surgeries, wrong site, 33
Sustain phase, 93
Sustainability, 127
Sustainment, 150
SWIP (Standard work in process),
    90, 154–155
Systems thinking, 61–74, 78, 91, 127,
    140, 150

T

Tables, 122
Takt time, 154
Teamwork, 91
Top-down implementation, 88
Total Preventive Maintenance
    (TPM), 90
Toyoda, Kiichiro, 95
Toyoda, Sakichi, 94
Toyota, 36, 39, 72, 95, 101, 140
Toyota Production System, 39, 72
Training, 101–102, 149–158
Transportation, 36, 39, 45, 130–131

U

Unobstructed throughput, 53, 54, 105
User-friendliness, 53, 54, 91, 92, 105

V

Value added activities, 160
Value stream, 104
Value stream focus, 104, 105
Value stream mapping, 90
Value stream maps (VSM), 142
Vancomycin-resistant enterococci
    (VRE), 33
Ventilator-associated pneumonia
    (VAP), 33, 68, 122, 173
Visual systems, 81–82, 163

VRE (Vancomycin-resistant
   enterococci), 33
VSM (Value stream maps), 142

W

Waiting, 36, 39, 41, 51, 59, 61
Waste
   defects, 39
   elimination, 90, 141

excessive motion, 39, 41, 42, 153
greatest, 151–153
inventory, 39, 58, 152, 155
as operation, 117
overprocessing, 39, 41
overproduction, 39, 58
transport, 36, 39, 45, 130–131
waiting, 36, 39, 41, 51, 59, 61
Welch, Jack, 170
Wright, Frank Lloyd, 163

About the Author

Tom Zidel is the president of Lean Hospitals, a consulting company that provides consulting, facilitation, and training exclusively to healthcare organizations. With more than 25 years of experience in Lean and Six Sigma implementation, Tom has guided many organizations on their Lean journey. He has dedicated the last 15 years to working exclusively with healthcare organizations. He is the author of the best-selling book *A Lean Guide to Transforming Healthcare: How to Implement Lean Principles in Hospitals, Medical Offices, Clinics and Other Healthcare Organizations* (2006). Tom has earned the prestigious Shingo Research and Professional Publication Award for his book *Lean Done Right: Achieve and Maintain Reform in Your Healthcare Organization* (2012), which was also a 2012 Axiom Business Book Awards silver medal winner in the category of operations management.

Tom has trained and/or mentored hundreds of healthcare professionals from many of our nation's leading hospitals, including Yale New Haven Health System, Johns Hopkins Hospital, and Aurora Health Care, in the use of Lean and

Six Sigma methods. He is a pioneer in Lean implementation in healthcare. His presentations and workshops are stimulating, energetic, and functional. His unique approach to Lean implementation allows organizations to sustain their Lean initiative by creating a Lean culture and systems thinking.

For Product Safety Concerns and Information please contact our EU
representative GPSR@taylorandfrancis.com
Taylor & Francis Verlag GmbH, Kaufingerstraße 24, 80331 München, Germany